Next door

— AS IT IS IN —

Heaven

LIVING OUT GOD'S KINGDOM
IN YOUR NEIGHBORHOOD

LANCE FORD & BRAD BRISCO

NAVPRESS

*A NavPress resource published in alliance
with Tyndale House Publishers, Inc.*

NAVPRESS ⬤®

NavPress is the publishing ministry of The Navigators, an international Christian organization and leader in personal spiritual development. NavPress is committed to helping people grow spiritually and enjoy lives of meaning and hope through personal and group resources that are biblically rooted, culturally relevant, and highly practical.

For more information, visit www.NavPress.com.

Next Door as It Is in Heaven: Living Out God's Kingdom in Your Neighborhood

Copyright © 2016 by Lance Ford and Brad Brisco. All rights reserved.

A NavPress resource published in alliance with Tyndale House Publishers, Inc.

NAVPRESS and the NAVPRESS logo are registered trademarks of NavPress, The Navigators, Colorado Springs, CO. *TYNDALE* is a registered trademark of Tyndale House Publishers, Inc. Absence of ® in connection with marks of NavPress or other parties does not indicate an absence of registration of those marks.

The Team:
Don Pape, Publisher; David Zimmerman, Acquiring Editor; Dan Farrell, Designer

Cover illustration copyright © CSA Images/Color Printstock Collection/Getty Images. All rights reserved.

Published in association with the literary agency of Mark Sweeney & Associates.

Some of the anecdotal illustrations in this book are true to life and are included with the permission of the persons involved. All other illustrations are composites of real situations, and any resemblance to people living or dead is coincidental.

Library of Congress Cataloging-in-Publication Data

Names: Ford, Lance, date, author.
Title: Next door as it is in heaven : living out God's kingdom in your neighborhood / Lance Ford and Brad Brisco.
Description: Colorado Springs : NavPress, 2016. | Includes bibliographical references. | Description based on print version record and CIP data provided by publisher; resource not viewed.
Identifiers: LCCN 2016017887 (print) | LCCN 2016015618 (ebook) | ISBN 9781631465000 (Apple) | ISBN 9781631464980 (E-Pub) | ISBN 9781631464997 (Kindle) | ISBN 9781631464973
Subjects: LCSH: Communities—Religious aspects—Christianity. | Neighborhoods.
Classification: LCC BV4517.5 (print) | LCC BV4517.5 .F67 2016 (ebook) | DDC 248.4—dc23
LC record available at https://lccn.loc.gov/2016017887

Printed in the United States of America

22   21   20   19   18   17   16
7   6   5   4   3   2   1

From Brad
To my father Billie Brisco.
Thanks for showing me
what it really means
to live for the sake of others.

From Lance
To the neighbors of my
childhood on Cherokee
Trail in Keller, Texas

Contents

There Goes the Neighborhood

It occurs to me that this is not a neighborhood;
it is only a collection of unconnected individuals.

PHILIP LANGDON, *A BETTER PLACE TO LIVE*

SOMETIMES OFFHANDED COMMENTS come across as back-handed compliments. What do you do when your young neighbor cheerfully says, "We love you guys! I always wanted to live next door to Fred and Ethel"?

What! Frumpy old Fred and matronly Ethel Mertz from *I Love Lucy*, the television classic that revolved around the lives of two neighborhood couples? Seriously, we remind you of them?

My first thought was that Hilary was calling us old. I know my wife and I (Lance) aren't exactly Brad and Angelina, but really? Come on. I'm cool. I'm in shape. And I'm not a penny pincher. Plus, I certainly don't hike my pants up past my belly button. And my wife, Sherri, is very fit and beautiful and . . .

Still, I knew what she meant. It was actually a compliment. Hilary was voicing good feelings about the friendships among a few of us neighbors by tapping into the nostalgia of days gone by. Heck, I want to live next to the Mertzes too.

Something has happened to the good old American neighborhood. It may be more accurate to say it *hasn't* happened. Most of us never experienced what Fred and Ethel and Lucy and Ricky experienced. The world of television and the movies is, for many people, their only experience of a community of connected friends and neighbors. Who wouldn't love to live in Beaver Cleaver's Mayfield or Andy Taylor's Mayberry—where you go to church with the same people you hang out with at the local barbershop or hair salon? Where you can stroll down to the only gas station in town for a bottle of pop with a group of friends? Or how about having a circle of friends in the city from a wide range of professions—blue collar to white collar—who hang out several times per week at a tavern named *Cheers*?

Those of us who grew up with these shows or ate breakfast in *Mr. Rogers' Neighborhood* when we were young, carry with us an unfulfilled longing for a neighborhood that actually works. We want to live across the hall from an entertaining neighbor personality like Chandler Bing or J. J. Evans, or on a street with neighbors named Martha, Ward, George Bailey, or Aunt Bee. We'd even welcome quirky neighbors like Cosmo Kramer or Steve Urkel. We long for a kitchen with a Dutch door where neighbors drop by and lean in to borrow a cup of sugar and talk about the weather. Or to stroll across the backyard in the evening to draw upon the wisdom of Wilson, our neighbor on the other side of the privacy fence, as we process a problem or crisis. I don't need a home where the buffalo roam. Give me a front porch with a swing and rocking chairs for friends and neighbors to serendipitously stop by to swap insights, opinions, dreams, and disappointments.

In recent years entrepreneurs, city planners, and real-estate developers have sought to tap into these subconscious desires. Howard Schultz, the visionary behind Starbucks, commenced building his espresso and coffee kingdom after visiting the quaint coffee shop culture of Italy. His imagination was captivated as he lingered in numerous shops with baristas who greeted patrons by name and knew their order without it being spoken. Schultz returned to Seattle with a desire to create a connecting point for community and conversation—a slowing-down place for people on the go to spend time with old friends and create new ones. Schultz's vision shaped coffee tastes across America but failed to deliver its original vision as a genuine hangout. For hangout purists, the addition of drive-through service was the ultimate sellout.

Suburban housing developers are attempting to recapture the ethos of what have become known as "walkable" neighborhoods. The objective is to include features that nurture relational connections. Seaside, Florida—which served as the backdrop for the Jim Carrey movie *The Truman Show*—and the Walt Disney Company's master-planned development of Celebration, Florida, are examples of communities developed with hopes of being a throwback to the town square, where retail shops and commercial enterprises can be reached from home on foot. With walking trails and sidewalks—elements widely forgotten by developers for decades—the idea is that people will naturally connect and build relationships through the frequency of day-to-day interaction. These communities are a reflection of what's been called the "new urbanism."

Given how much value we place on neighbor relationships in our media and marketing, why do such relationships seem so old-fashioned? Immediately following World War II an increasing demand for affordable housing by a suddenly prosperous American citizenship and returning GIs produced the first suburban neighborhoods. America had become an automobile culture, and planners designed new housing developments with this in mind. Levittown, New York, is widely considered the first postwar suburban housing development, setting a pattern for thousands to follow. In recent years, critics of the modern suburb model have pointed to the lack of elements that foster natural interaction among residents. Besides the push indoors from air conditioning, television, and the Internet, neighborhoods suffer from a lack of commercial enterprises, sacrificed on the altar of zoning laws. To purchase even the smallest food or medicinal item, residents must drive out of their neighborhood. There is no corner pub or coffee shop within walking distance where they might spend time around a drink with their neighbors. Long gone are the days where folks waved from their front porches or made small talk as their neighbors passed by on the way to the corner drugstore or butcher shop. Those destinations have been written out of the neighborhood.

The notion of a neighborhood church has almost completely disappeared, and with it, the concept of *parish*—a body of Christians who live in proximity to one another and sense a call and privileged duty to care for one another. In all but rare cases, church members now drive to church services from all over a city. Few members of any given church live in proximity to one another as neighbors. This means the church you are a member of consists mostly of people you don't do day-to-day life with.

National surveys reveal that less than half the American populace knows most of their neighbors' names. It is sad to consider that many people live for years in an apartment complex or neighborhood without so much as knowing their neighbors.

What does all this neighborhood business have to do with the gospel? How is it connected with the kingdom of God? As Jesus followers—people of the Good News—we follow the one who said the most important commandment is to love God with all our heart, soul, and strength, and to love our neighbors as ourselves. We have a tremendous opportunity before us: to take notice and help to resurrect rich relationships in our neighborhoods.

But too often that opportunity is left untaken. Jay Pathak and Dave Runyon relate their collective horror and embarrassment when a city official said to them and a group of their fellow Denver area pastors, "From the city's perspective, there isn't a noticeable difference in how Christians and non-Christians neighbor in our community."[1]

Let that sink in. If anyone should "neighbor" differently, it should be us. So let's do it. Let us love our neighborhoods as ourselves.

As you traverse the pages ahead, keep in mind your particular context: where you live, work, eat, and play on a regular basis. The Holy Spirit has sent every Christian to those places. It is no accident that you live where you do, even if it is temporary. Moving through the book, you will gain an understanding not only of the needs around you but also, happily, of the resources and ability to meet those needs. You'll also have great fun and joy along the journey, as you discover that there are others all around you who desire to see the neighborhood come alive in rich relationships as well.

Place Matters

THE PRIORITY OF INCARNATIONAL PRESENCE

There's no place like home. There's no place like home.
There's no place like home.
DOROTHY, THE WIZARD OF OZ

To be a stranger in a strange land, to be lost . . . is perhaps
the condition most typical of contemporary life.
IAIN CHAMBERS

Being rooted is perhaps the least recognized and most
important need of humans.
WENDELL BERRY

Seek the welfare of the city where I have sent you into exile,
and pray to the LORD on its behalf, for in its welfare
you will find your welfare.
JEREMIAH 29:7, ESV

THE 1990 FILM *AVALON,* directed by Barry Levinson, begins on the Fourth of July, 1914. Sam Krichinsky, one of four brothers who eventually relocate from Russia to America, arrives in the Baltimore neighborhood of Avalon. Gradually, the other Krichinskys arrive, pooling their resources to bring over more and more family members. Each new member settles in Avalon and joins the ever-expanding network of relationships.

The first half of the film highlights the integration of the extended family. There are scenes of siblings and numerous cousins playing in the streets between the Baltimore row houses. Mothers talk with each other across front porches, asking when their neighbor will be walking to the nearby market and whether they might walk together. Children are seen with not only parents but also grandparents, aunts, and uncles who either live in the same house or nearby. The weekly family dinner becomes so large that several tables have to be put end to end to accommodate everyone for the shared meal.

Avalon begins as a portrait of a robust, relationally rich extended family. Life is lived *with* others, both in times of shared joy and in periods of struggles and hardships. People are connected. Conversations are many. Common meals are the norm. Life is rooted not only in relationships with others but also in relationship to place.

About halfway into the film, however, something begins to change. The vibrant colors begin to darken. The mood of the story changes. Three forces are introduced into the life of Avalon that fragment the characters' relational connectedness. At first hardly anyone notices. The changes seem natural—even commendable. But once the family fully embraces the modern American way of living, there is no possibility of holding the pieces together.

The three separate but interconnected themes introduced into the life of the Krichinsky family include the creation of suburbs, the rise of the automobile, and the popularization of television. While each of these issues leads to a similar outcome, in regards to the fragmentation of their extended family, they each take a slightly different route toward the transformation.

The creation of the suburbs. The second generation of the Krichinsky family is experiencing the upward mobility of a postwar economic boom, with the accompanying (false) promise of a better life. More conveniences. More leisure. More space. In one poignant scene, Sam's grandson Michael (played by a young Elijah Wood) learns that his family will be moving away from the rest of the relatives, out to this new world called the suburbs. "What's a suburb?" he asks.

His mother replies, "It's a nicer place to live."

"That's what it means?" he counters. "A nicer place? Everyone is going to live there too, right? In one house?"

In the mind of this young boy, the thought of moving away from a permanent, familiar place full of relationships cultivated over a lifetime simply didn't make sense.

The rise of the automobile. As automobiles became more affordable and thus more common, fathers were able to relocate their families to the suburbs without giving up their jobs in Avalon. Every day they would drive out of the neighborhood, alone, to work in a place that was no longer home. In some cases, the places they lived were so far away that fathers were late coming home, missing time with their children.

The popularization of television. Just when the family is about to eat dinner together at the dining room table, they realize their favorite television program is about to come on.

They all grab their plates and rush into the living room, where they sit silently, staring at the television. Smaller groups eating off TV trays replace the large, loud family meal. Family conversations about the specifics of the day are left behind.

The final sequence in *Avalon* is heartbreaking. Sam, now in the final years of life, sits by himself, late at night. Asleep in his recliner, alone in the living room with little more than his chair and a television, he sits in a room gone dark except for the dim light that radiates from the television. The broadcast day has ended.

When viewing the film for the first time, I (Brad) recognized the significant similarities the movie had with a book published the same year by sociologist Ray Oldenburg. In *The Great Good Place*, Oldenburg contends that the vast majority of communities in the United States are void of relational vitality—primarily because of the loss of what he calls informal public places. Oldenburg understands the absence of this informal public life as being the result of suburban sprawl and the rise of the automobile culture, both of which foster geographical and relational separation between home and workplace.

Magnifying the problem is the proliferation of home entertainment that often inhibits face-to-face communication. This has, of course, moved far beyond the simple introduction of television as portrayed in the film. Today smartphones, computers, gaming devices, and limitless television viewing options get between us and the people closest to us.

The combination of these factors is pushing individuals toward what Oldenburg calls "pitiable isolation," prohibiting sufficient opportunities and encouragement for voluntary human interaction. He describes daily life in the typical suburban setting as being like "a grammar school without its recess periods" or "incurring the aches and pains of a softball game without the fun of getting together for a few beers afterwards."[1] Both the joy of hanging out with people and the social cohesion that comes from it are disappearing; the settings to make them possible are fading away.

> The problem of place in America manifests itself in a sorely deficient informal public life. The structure of shared experience beyond that offered by family, job, and passive consumerism is small and dwindling. The essential group experience is being replaced by the exaggerated self-consciousness of individuals. American life-styles, for all the material acquisition and the seeking after comforts and pleasures, are plagued by boredom, loneliness, alienation, and a high price tag. America can point to many areas where she has made progress, but in the area of informal public life she has lost ground and continues to lose it.[2]

The warning that Oldenburg was sounding more than twenty-five years ago is as pertinent as ever. Today we recognize that his proposal was just the tip of the iceberg. The demise of relational vitality that Oldenburg described is feeble compared to the level of displacement and personal isolation felt by many today. Even though there has been a deliberate upswing in the establishment of public places (which we will discuss in chapter 8), that trend continues to fight against new forces of relational isolation.

Look at All the Lonely People

God created us as social, relational beings. We are made to be in relationship both with the Creator and with other people. We have been formed with an innate need to know and be known. Yet the current way of life in developed countries is greatly reducing the quantity and quality of our relationships. The majority of people no longer live among or even near their extended families. Instead, people often live on the other side of the country or even across the world from their relatives. When you add the high degree of mobility, the strong sense of individualism, and the decreased opportunities for informal public life, isolation and loneliness become increasingly common.

Studies show that we are now actually "connected" to a larger and more diverse circle of people. Even so, nearly a quarter of Americans say they have nobody to talk to, up from 8 percent in 1985.[3] And this is not simply a picture of solitary retirees. The middle-aged are the loneliest group of all in the United States. According to one recent study, 40 percent of adults between the ages of forty-five and forty-nine said they were lonely, a rate of loneliness that has doubled since the 1980s.[4]

The National Science Foundation has discovered that the number of Americans' quality connections had taken a dive in the past two decades. They asked thousands of people of all ages, "Who are the people with whom you discussed important matters over the last six months?" In 1985 Americans had an average of three confidants. By 2004 they had fewer than two.[5] One in four said that they had *no one* whom they could talk to about personal "troubles or triumphs."[6] If family members were not counted, that number doubled: More than half of those surveyed had no one outside their immediate family with whom they could share important issues. In short, we have fewer people to lean on.

Let's make this more personal. Stop for a moment and reflect on the people you come in contact with on a regular basis. Almost half of them have, at best, one person they can talk to about important topics. Do you get the sense that the researchers are right? What about the divorced man who lives across the street? Or the widow in the apartment next door? The young single mom who works behind the checkout counter? The college student, far from home, who waits tables at your favorite restaurant? In nearly every American setting, people are indeed living relationally impoverished lives marked by a sense of isolation. Far too many people are alone and lonely.

The issue of isolation is compounded by a sense of detachment from place. In a highly mobile society, people rarely feel rooted geographically. We live as nomads, both figuratively and literally. The authors of *Beyond Homelessness: Christian Faith in a Culture of Displacement* are concerned about a "culture-wide attitude" characterized by the phrase "This world is not my home—I'm just passing through":

Whether we are talking about the upwardly mobile who view each place as a rung in the ladder that goes up to who knows where, or the postmodern nomad with no roots in any place or any tradition of place, or the average consumer who doesn't know anything about the place where she lives or the places her food comes from, the reality is the same—we are a culture of displacement. . . .

Wanderer, expatriate, exile, diaspora, stranger, migrancy, displacement—all ways to describe the homelessness of the late twentieth century and early twenty-first century.[7]

In his book *Incarnate*, author Michael Frost uses the term *excarnation* to describe this idea of displacement. Excarnation, meaning "to deflesh," is the opposite of the theological term *incarnation* ("to take on flesh"; see John 1:14). Frost compares the modern Western experience of life to that of a tourist, someone who is always moving, never belonging. Always interested in collecting experiences, but remaining superficial and disconnected from permanency. Moreover, when the physical places we inhabit—our homes, offices, shopping malls, highways, airports, cities—all look alike, place seems to matter even less. We end up with what James Howard Kunstler calls "the geography of nowhere."[8] Our culture becomes rootless and disengaged, both relationally and in regard to corporal place.[9]

This lack of meaningful social interaction and sense of

displacement is not only heartbreaking—because we were created for so much more—but astoundingly harmful to our way of life. It is literally killing us. According to the volume of evidence Susan Pinker assembles in her book *The Village Effect*, persistent loneliness alters the genes in every cell of our bodies. And not in a good way.

Presenting data from numerous studies, Pinker offers a compelling argument that the strength of our social relationships is comparable to well-established risk factors for mortality such as smoking and alcohol consumption. Weak social relationships are a more significant risk factor than physical inactivity and obesity. Simply playing cards once a week or meeting friends every Wednesday night at Starbucks, she shows, adds as many years to our lives as taking beta-blockers or quitting a pack-a-day smoking habit. The subtitle of Pinker's book, *How Face-to-Face Contact Can Make Us Healthier, Happier, and Smarter*, gets the point across: If we don't interact regularly with people face-to-face, the odds are that we won't live as long, remember information as well, or be as happy as we otherwise could have been.

Word Became Flesh and Blood

What is the appropriate response to a culture of increasing displacement? Can something really be done to turn the tide of isolation? Are there practical actions that can be taken to help mend the broken pieces? To restore people *and* places back to a point where they can once again flourish?

The solution is no doubt multifaceted. It will involve a variety of tactics, including the themes spelled out in the remaining pages of this book: the art of neighboring, restoring genuine community, sharing meals with others, welcoming the stranger, and opening our lives to those who are disconnected. But we are convinced that every practical action—the "how"—must be rooted in the "why" of *incarnational presence*. The journey of restoring the relational fabric of our communities must begin with our tangible presence in *real time* and *real space*.

When we use the language of incarnational presence we are referring to the incarnation of Jesus. The word *incarnation* refers to the act whereby God took it upon himself to enter into the depths of our world, for the purpose of reconciling humanity back to himself. The incarnation is thus God's ultimate missional participation in creation (John 3:16-17).

It is interesting to note the integral part that public spaces of first-century Palestine played in Jesus' ministry on earth. When God entered into our world, in and through the person of Jesus, he came to live among us (*eskenosen*—literally, "set up a tent"). As Eugene Peterson renders John 1:14 in *The Message*, "The Word became flesh and blood, and moved into the neighborhood." As Eric Jacobsen writes:

> Certainly, Jesus spent time in the private spaces of other people's homes. He also ministered in the semiprivate realm of temple and synagogue. But by

and large, most of his ministry took place in public spaces, where he risked relationship with people he didn't know and interacted with them on neutral territory.[10]

The incarnation of Jesus should inform our activity in the world. Alan Hirsch reminds us that "if God's central way of reaching his world was to incarnate himself in Jesus, then our way of reaching the world should likewise be incarnational."[11] The Christian faith is a faith that is always *placed*—in creation, in history, in time. And it continues to be a faith of embodied presence.

Simon Carey Holt, in his excellent book *God Next Door: Spirituality and Mission in the Neighbourhood*, roots the Incarnation in the Christian story of place.

The truth is we are not created to be placeless wanderers. The Garden of Eden, the promised land, the city on a hill, the house with many rooms, the streets of gold: the Christian story is a story of places—the most tangible places—from beginning to end. We are made to inhabit. Even the missionary who treks half way around the world does so to settle somewhere in particular and there to dwell for the sake of the gospel. The story of the incarnation is the story of God en-fleshed in a particular place at a particular time and within a very specific community. So too for us, the call of God is to be in

a particular place and there to embody the presence
and grace of God. It's a call to locality.[12]

Both presence and place matter. If there is any possibility for human flourishing in a dislocated, isolated world,
it begins when God's love is embodied in us and enacted
through us. Just as God took on flesh in the person of Jesus
in order to dwell among us and to identify with us, we as the
body of Christ are to incarnate into the places we live.

Going below the Surface

Our friend Jon Huckins cowrote a book titled *Thin Places*,
in which he uses the language of *submerging* to describe our
incarnational posture toward the places we live. Growing up
on the West Coast, Jon shares his lifelong love for the ocean.
As much as he loves the view of the expansive body of water,
his favorite aspect of the ocean is stepping into it. Whether
he is surfing, snorkeling, or simply swimming, the ocean tells
a completely different story when he steps into it and allows
it to surround him.

A body of water that appears tamed by the constructs
of the surrounding shorelines becomes a mysterious
and vibrant playground for forms of life that I otherwise would never know existed. It is as though I see
the ocean for the very first time once I submerge. And
ultimately, what I see from below is much more true

of its identity than what I see from above as a passive observer. . . . Much of the same realities are true in our submerging posture. . . . When we submerge into our context, we see that the story we have been told to believe about our neighbors, politics, and economy is far from reality.[13]

Submerging is a good metaphor for incarnational living. Only when we go below the surface of our neighborhoods are we able to move from being disengaged observers to active citizens.

Seeking the Welfare of *Your* City

There is a fascinating passage in the Old Testament that provides a picture of what it looks like to live out incarnational presence. It actually gives practical instructions for digging into the places we live. It is especially helpful when Christians sense they are living in a world that is hostile toward their beliefs, or perhaps when we find ourselves living in a place that doesn't really feel like home.

In the prophetic book of Jeremiah, we read how the nation of Israel had forsaken God's law and, as a result, found themselves taken into captivity and exiled far from their Jerusalem homeland. God had sent the Babylonian empire to discipline his people. As they were relocated to a foreign, idolatrous land, they began to hear that their time there would be short. False prophets were telling the nation of Israel that God would soon deliver them and that settling into this new, strange land was foolish. God's Word through the prophet Jeremiah to the exiles was quite different.

> Thus says the LORD of hosts, the God of Israel,
> to all the exiles whom I have sent into exile from
> Jerusalem to Babylon: Build houses and live in them;
> plant gardens and eat their produce. Take wives and
> have sons and daughters; take wives for your sons,
> and give your daughters in marriage, that they may
> bear sons and daughters; multiply there, and do not
> decrease. But seek the welfare of the city where I
> have sent you into exile, and pray to the LORD on its
> behalf, for in its welfare you will find your welfare.
>
> JEREMIAH 29:4-7, ESV

The words of Jeremiah were shocking. The premise of his message was that the exiles would be in Babylon for several generations—at least seventy years, a time period that included not only the reign of King Nebuchadnezzar but of his son and grandson (Jeremiah 25:11; 27:7; 29:10), and that the Israelites would simply need to come to terms with this fact. God was telling them to settle down and get used to being in this hostile, ungodly place.

It was toward this end that Jeremiah counseled his community not to be nostalgic for the past, for the past could not be recovered. Nor did he advise them

to plan for insurrection, for there was no promise
of their restoration in Jerusalem, at least not any
time soon. Nor yet was the community's survival
tied to the remnant that remained in Jerusalem (Jer.
24:5-10). For Jeremiah, exile did not mean that
God had abandoned Israel. Rather, exile was the
place where God was at work. God's purposes with
Israel, in other words, were served by the Babylonian
invasion.[14]

Jeremiah's instructions were more counterintuitive than
they might at first seem. Jeremiah tells the Jews in exile to "seek
the welfare" of their captors, to pray for the very people who
destroyed their homeland, because the welfare of the exiles
and the captors were bound together.[15] If God's purposes with
Israel were really being fulfilled through their captivity, then as
the exiles pursued the shalom of the home of their captors—
Babylon—God would provide shalom for those in exile.

It would have seemed reasonable for the Jews to be hostile
to their captors.[16] It also would have been natural for them to
withdraw from the world around them. By the same token,
it would have been easy for them to simply assimilate with
the culture that surrounded them. Any of these three options
would have made sense in human terms. However, God was
calling the Israelites to something radically different—not
to be defensive *against*, isolated *from*, or absorbed *into* the
dominant culture, but instead to be incarnated *within* it.[17]
He was calling them to dig into the place that he had sent

them, to stay where they would be doing life for a long time. He was calling them to submerge.

Furthermore, what God instructed the exiles to *do* is actually rather ordinary. Consider the list from Jeremiah 29:

- Build houses and live in them
- Plant gardens and eat their produce
- Have children
- Marry off your children so they have children
- Seek the welfare of the city
- Pray for the welfare of the city

There is nothing in this list that is dramatic or miraculous. It is a list of normal, everyday activities. It could represent any person, regardless of income, social status, education, vocation, or geographical location. The way the kingdom of God takes root in the lives of people and ultimately changes a city is by exiles living normal, everyday lives as citizens of the King in every neighborhood and public place that makes up a city. We build houses. We plant gardens. We have children. We seek the welfare of our city. Far more often than not, the ways of Jesus are indeed local and ordinary.

Jeremiah 29 coheres well with what we read throughout the New Testament. Peter speaks of Christians as "elect exiles of the Dispersion" (1 Peter 1:1, ESV) and "as aliens" (2:11, NASB). He encourages his readers to live "in reverent fear" during "your time as foreigners" (1:17). He urges believers repeatedly to do good (3:17) and for each person to use their gifts "to serve others, as faithful stewards of God's grace" (4:10). This also aligns with Paul's admonitions to "never tire of doing what is good" (2 Thessalonians 3:13), to "let your gentleness be evident to all" (Philippians 4:5), and to look to each other's interests and not merely to their own (Philippians 2:4). As Paul writes elsewhere, "Now to each one the manifestation of the Spirit is given for the common good" (1 Corinthians 12:7). James Davison Hunter sees each of these New Testament instructions as being "in keeping with the instruction that the people of God are to be committed to the welfare of the cities in which they reside in exile, even when the city is indifferent, hostile, or ungrateful."[18]

Are you willing to commit to the welfare of *your* city? Will you allow your imagination to see a movement that begins with the local and ordinary but over time becomes global and extraordinary? If your answer is yes, then together let's seek the welfare of our neighborhoods, and then let us strive for it to spill over into every nook and cranny of our city. Let's dig in, incarnate into the places we are already doing life, and display to a fragmented and isolated world a new way to be human.

Reflection and Preparation

Immerse. Read Jeremiah 29:4-7. Reflect on the list of actions God was telling the exiles to do: build houses and live in them, plant gardens and eat their produce, have children, marry off your children so they have children, seek the welfare of the city, and pray for the welfare of the city. How do you see each of these instructions fitting the theme of incarnational presence shared in this chapter?

Consider others. What are the implications of each of these in regards to daily living? How does each of these actions apply to you today? In what practical ways can you seek the welfare of your city? How can you lead others to do the same?

Pray. Begin by praying for the welfare of your city. Where are the broken places that need to be restored? Pray for those places. Who are the people who are most affected by the broken systems in your city? Pray for those systems. Pray for those people.

- 2 -
The Real Neighbor

OPEN HEARTS, OPEN DOORS

You'll be known as those who can fix anything,
restore old ruins, rebuild and renovate,
make the community livable again.

ISAIAH 58:9-12, MSG

MY SATURDAY MORNING golf outing was placed on pause. I (Lance) was sitting in a golf cart; my wife (Sherri) was on the other end of the phone. "I don't know what to do for her," my wife sniffled. "I don't even know her name."

Our peaceful weekend morning had come undone by the sound of cries from the house beside ours. It was springtime, and with windows open, it was impossible for my wife not to overhear the shouting match that had erupted. It was the young wife's birthday, and her husband had just loaded his boat and left for a fishing trip with his buddies. The young woman couldn't believe her newlywed husband had not planned to spend the day with her. And now Sherri was crying because she was trying.

"Well, I don't know what to do," I told her. "If I knew him I would try to thump a little advice into him on how to be a decent husband."

Sherri wanted to do something—anything—to help, so she decided to send the young woman an anonymous bouquet of flowers with a card that said, "Happy Birthday. Know you are loved."

That was eighteen years ago. We had not yet learned a lot about making a neighborhood livable. I am ashamed to say it, but we were too busy planting a church and raising our kids to view our neighborhood as a place to which we were called by the Lord and sent directly to reach and make better. We chose to live in our neighborhood based on how it would serve our personal wants and needs. We failed to realize that opportunities to bring something better to our neighbors and have our own lives affected were all around us. We primarily viewed our presence in the neighborhood as about us.

But I remember thinking about how differently this neighbor crisis was playing out in comparison to something similar I was privy to as a child. Countless times growing up in a middle-class suburban neighborhood in the mid-1970s, I had been shooed out of the house so my parents could talk our neighbors through a spat or crisis. My mom and dad were in their midforties and had been married long enough to play the role of elders to the younger couple. They had become surrogate counselors for Dan and Jenny.

Momma taught Jenny how to sew and sharpen her cooking skills. Daddy spent countless hours with Dan, working on cars or just sitting in lawn chairs in our front yard, fretting about the lowly Texas Rangers and talking about parenting, husbanding, and the joys and struggles of figuring out life. My dad could see that Dan was headed down the same path he had taken in his younger years. An affection for Lone Star beer was destroying his marriage. From personal experience, my dad was able to call it like he saw it with Dan while showing him a better way—the good news of the gospel. Along the journey, both Jenny and Dan became believers in Jesus, and my folks began informally discipling them.

My parents were raised in an era when neighbors actually knew one another. I am still baffled by the fact that one of my parents' first dwellings included a shared bathroom situated between two apartments. According to my mom, it was not that uncommon back in the day. Contrast that to nowadays, where it is not unusual for people to live next door to one another—for years in some cases—without even knowing each other's names.

Every so often we witness the extreme of this phenomenon, as a news story surfaces about a deceased person being discovered in a home or apartment, having been dead for months or even years. With no pattern of regular interaction, neighbors went on with their lives, not noticing the "missing" person. The person's death was missed because his or her life was missed.

Heaven on Earth

The business of neighboring was enormously important to Jesus. He was the consummate people person, and he gave his followers a clear mandate on the matter.

Jesus was frequently cajoled and pestered by religious leaders attempting to trap him in theological arguments. One day one of these guys got more than he bargained for when he asked Jesus how he could inherit eternal life. It was almost as if he was just waiting for that question. A thought bubble above Jesus may have said, "I'm so glad you asked."

> And behold, a lawyer stood up to put him to the test, saying, "Teacher, what shall I do to inherit eternal life?" He said to him, "What is written in the Law? How do you read it?" And he answered, "You shall love the Lord your God with all your heart and with all your soul and with all your strength and with all your mind, and your neighbor as yourself." And he said to him, "You have answered correctly; do this, and you will live."
>
> But he, desiring to justify himself, said to Jesus, "And who is my neighbor?"
>
> LUKE 10:25-29, ESV

In their outstanding book *The Art of Neighboring*, Jay Pathak and Dave Runyon discuss the parable of the Good Samaritan that follows this passage, and the temptation to generalize the concept of *neighbor* to the extent that, in practice, we never encounter an actual neighbor:

> If we say, "Everyone is my neighbor," it can become an excuse for avoiding the implications of following the Great Commandment. Our "neighbors" become defined in the broadest of terms. They're the people across town, the people who are helped by the organizations that receive our donations, the people whom the government helps. We don't have to feel guilty, we tell ourselves. After all, we can't be expected to really love everybody, can we?
>
> The problem is, however, that when we aim for everything, we hit nothing. So when we insist we're neighbors with everybody, often we end up being neighbors with nobody. . . . We become like the lawyer looking for a loophole. We tell ourselves that we've got a lot going on in our lives, so surely the Great Commandment applies only to the wounded enemy lying beside the road, doesn't it? Since we haven't come across many of those lately, surely we're doing just fine when it comes to loving our neighbors.
>
> Maybe not.[1]

The religionist who asked Jesus about eternity didn't have a problem with Jesus' answer—up to a point. It is just that last little bit—"and your neighbor as yourself"—he wanted clarity on. But his motives were clear: Luke says he wanted to justify himself. To do so he needed to keep the definition of *neighbor* in the realm of the ethereal. This part must stay mystical. It cannot become actual. To go literal with this idea of loving our neighbor would be too invasive and impractical. These must only be theological "beliefs" to be agreed with, not real-world commandments to be practiced.

It is easy for anyone to claim that she loves God with her all and all, because God is unseen. How can you tell whether a person really loves God or not? This is the problem our flesh usually has with Jesus. He actually means what he says. So the questioner wants him to define *neighbor*. Jesus is more than happy to oblige.

> Jesus replied, "A man was going down from Jerusalem to Jericho, and he fell among robbers, who stripped him and beat him and departed, leaving him half dead. Now by chance a priest was going down that road, and when he saw him he passed by on the other side. So likewise a Levite, when he came to the place and saw him, passed by on the other side. But a Samaritan, as he journeyed, came to where he was, and when he saw him, he had compassion. He went to him and bound up his wounds, pouring on oil and wine. Then he set him on his own animal and brought him to an inn and took care of him. And the next day he took out two denarii and gave them to the innkeeper, saying,

'Take care of him, and whatever more you spend,
I will repay you when I come back.' Which of these
three, do you think, proved to be a neighbor to the
man who fell among the robbers?" He said, "The
one who showed him mercy." And Jesus said to him,
"You go, and do likewise."

LUKE 10:30-37, ESV

Now the guy is really in a pickle. Jesus says the question we must ask is not "Who is my neighbor?" because if that were the case, then we could pick and choose who gets our love. We could go about our days qualifying or disqualifying who is eligible or deserving of it. Jesus says we must ask ourselves, "Am *I* a neighbor?"

We are struck with the classic wisdom Jesus expressed in this passage. The characters in the parable are two top-of-the-religious-heap guys (a priest and a Levite) and a bottom-of-the-heap Samaritan—the most despised person in the eyes of the religious Jewish elite.

Let's not miss the point that this entire scene unfolded when the theologian asked Jesus how a person finds eternal life. The almost exclusive understanding or assumption of this passage is that the lawyer was asking, "How do I get into heaven when I die?" If that were indeed the question, however, then Jesus would be giving a formula on how to earn our salvation; the Cross would not even have been necessary.

No, the question is "How do I enter into eternal *life* right now?" The Greek word for "life" here, *zoé*, means life that is real and genuine—life in its fullness and vitality. Jesus is all about that very point. In verse 28 he tells the guy, "Do this and you will *live*," which is a slight iteration of *zoé*. The word "eternal" in front of *zoé* speaks to the source: Eternal life is life with heaven as its source. Jesus is giving us the keys to experiencing heavenly life right here, right now.

It wasn't the pious guys in the parable that had eternal life. Far from it. It was the plain old Samaritan, down at the bottom of the religious ladder, who demonstrated he had a handle on what it means to live out love for God by loving others.

The Real Neighbor

As followers of Jesus, we can't afford to miss the point in this legendary parable. We believe we would better understand Jesus' point if, rather than calling this familiar story "the parable of the Good Samaritan," we called it "the parable of the real neighbor." The Samaritan—the one who proved to be a real neighbor—demonstrates several important traits we can learn from.

Nearing. First, unlike the priest and the Levite who came upon the victim and intentionally crossed the street, the Samaritan moved in closer to assess what looked to be a bad circumstance. All three of the players in Jesus' story "saw" the man who was in distress. All three of these guys were busy. They were on a journey. They had things to do. People to see. They were carrying on the duties and business of life. But there was a difference in the three. Two people saw and went *on*. One person saw and went *to*.

It is so much easier to just "pass over to the other side." What we thought we saw or heard may not be the case. It could just be our imagination. That conversation I overheard between one of my kids and her playmate from down the street may have *sounded* like her family is struggling with finances, but I may have misunderstood. Then again, little Carly does seem to eagerly accept every offer for a snack or to stay for dinner.

I see our elderly neighbor across the street mowing his lawn, so I guess he is up to the task. I wonder if it would be a blessing to him if I offered to do that, or is the exercise good for him? Does he enjoy doing it himself? I will never know the answer unless, like the Good Samaritan, I go *to* the person. If I "pass by on the other side," as the priest and Levite did, I will never know for sure.

Caring. The *real* neighbor in Jesus' story begins to attend to the wounds he discovers. Not only does he offer his own immediate resources, he seeks the assistance of others nearby. The Samaritan needed to continue his journey. But he didn't just leave the man behind. He asked an innkeeper to take care of the fallen man. He said, "I'll pay for his lodging and any other expenses, but this person needs more than that. Will you join me and pitch in and care for him while I am away?" Think about that. It is not normal for an innkeeper to play nursemaid to a houseguest, but the Samaritan made the request anyway. Our aim must be higher than just to be a good neighbor ourselves. The goal is to create a *neighborhood* of good neighbors whereby the collective gifts, talents, resources, and caring hearts of many neighbors join forces when needs arise.

Sharing. Finally, look back and see what set this neighboring example in motion. Before we get the parable of the real neighbor, we get the great commandment: "You shall love the Lord your God with all your heart and with all your soul and with all your strength and with all your mind." Heart. Soul. Strength. Mind. Jesus is talking about our passion and being. He is talking about our hearts, our hands, and our heads. What do you care deeply about? What do you love to do? What is your passion? What are you skilled at and knowledgeable about? Jesus says, "Love God with all of that!" And then he says, "Make it tangible by loving your neighbor as yourself."

When we are passionate about something, we want others to experience it as we have. Think about it. What is one of the first things you do after you have watched a movie you really liked? You tell your friends, "Oh, you *have* to go see it. It's incredible!" It's the same with a great book or a newly discovered restaurant or recipe. Some people do this with a new tool, a new app, or a new electronic device they have discovered. "I heard you are putting in a new wood floor this weekend. You are welcome to use my compound miter saw. It's great. It has a laser guide and auto measuring. I'll bring it over!"

It is natural for us to share what we have and know with *friends*. But Jesus takes it to an entirely different level. He defines real neighbors as those who are willing to do so with strangers—and not just strangers because they've never met. Jesus stretches the possibilities beyond the limits of comfort. He takes it to the extreme. By choosing a Samaritan as the real neighbor, while using a priest and a Levite as the failed neighbors in his story, Jesus blows away all excuses for ignoring our call to being neighbors.

No Neighbors, No Neighborhood

Two of the most important initiating principles for neighboring are to (1) take notice and (2) invite others to join you. For a neighborhood to flourish, it takes a joint effort of people who care about their neighbors and their neighborhood. Besides being essential, however, this joint effort is fun and brings joy to all who are involved. It manifests and takes us into real life— eternal life. It is how we make a neighborhood worth living in.

When Ali Ebright moved into the neighborhood in Kansas City, Missouri, known as River Market, she was eager for a genuine sense of community. In her previous neighborhood she had a few friends and had gotten to know a few neighbors, but she yearned for something deeper. Ali wondered how she could help to make a piece of geography with disconnected inhabitants into a neighborhood of caring friends. Being a full-time food blogger, she decided to start with what she had—what she knew about and what she could do. She would start with food.

Recruiting a few neighbors she had met, Ali launched

"Neighbor Nights." Two years later, these Tuesday evening gatherings have become a weekly event on the calendar for three dozen or more residents in the neighborhood. When the weather is nice, they meet around a common area with picnic table and grill. She even talked the landlord of her building into donating the grill. On other nights, meals are shared at a local restaurant or through progressive dinners. The impact of Neighbor Nights has been, in a word, incredible. This is no "eat and run" affair. Over the last two years, residents have become *friends*. Liam, the neighborhood dog whisperer, reports that neighbors here watch each other's pets when they have to be away for extended times. Cynthia, an NN regular, says, "We look out for each other. We have keys for each other's places. This just took off."

In the midst of Ali's neighborhood is Quay Coffee, which she says primed the pump for Neighbor Nights. It served as a neutral hangout where neighbors began to notice one another as regulars, striking up conversations that evolved into friendships and community. But it took someone to get the ball rolling. Ali was that person. Her hunch was that she was not alone in the desire for connecting in meaningful neighboring relationships. But she knew she couldn't do it alone. So she invited others to join her as a core group of collaborators.

Full Circle

At the beginning of this chapter, I (Lance) shared about my parents and their neighborhood. Fast-forward thirty years.

By this time my folks were in their seventies; neither one of them was in the best of health. Living over six hundred miles away from them, I was constantly concerned with their well-being. But my anxiety was greatly reduced because of some *real* neighbors.

On one side of my folks' house lived the Dunham sisters. They had grown up next door to my parents and inherited their parents' home. If a day or two went by where Kim and Nancy did not notice my dad sitting at his lawn chair, listening to a ball game or sports radio, they would call or knock on the door to make sure everything was all right. Kim was a nurse, and from time to time she would check my parents' blood pressure and listen to their hearts to make sure all was well. Kim, Nancy, and I all had one another's phone numbers; the night my mom suffered a stroke, my dad called Kim over, and Kim reached me from the hospital. She had driven my father there as they followed the ambulance carrying my mother.

On the other side of my folks' home were the Espinosas. Steve and Dana had lived there for several years, and my parents had become grandparent figures for their children. The entire Espinosa family loved my mom and dad, and they showed it. Steve and one of their sons mowed my folks' yard, refusing to be paid. (They gladly accepted Momma's amazing homemade pies from time to time.) Dana helped my mother to understand the occasional bill she had trouble reading or to avoid the "incredible once-in-a-lifetime" scams aimed at unsuspecting senior citizens. Steve even added a gate between their backyards, so that my parents could come over to visit them around their swimming pool.

The stories we have shared in this chapter are of ordinary people doing ordinary things but getting extraordinary results. Something noteworthy stands out when we consider real neighboring. It creates the most robust and vigorous essence of life, all the while not requiring some enormous skillset or laborious undertaking. It just takes a willingness to adopt a handful of habits that any of us can take on.

As we move forward you will read several more such stories and have your imagination piqued as to what can happen in your own neighborhood. You will meet moms, mechanics, bartenders, baristas, bicycle repairmen, and retirees. Along with neighboring lessons from schoolteachers, seminary professors, artists, and architects, we will share stories from young mothers who work at home as well as those who have daily commutes. These are everyday people from across the social fields who have one thing in common: They are deeply engaged in shaping their neighborhoods and have learned to do so from nothing but passion and love. You will see how a love for the gospel and obedience to Jesus' commandment to love our neighbor as ourselves result in whole communities experiencing the people of God being salt and light.

People living all around us—on our block or in our apartment building—are waiting for someone to get things going. Will you be that person? Who will join you? If they could muster the courage or know how to say it, many of your neighbors would ask what the Reverend Mr. Fred Rogers sang to many of us who watched him daily in our childhood: "Won't you be my neighbor?"

Reflection and Preparation

Immerse. Slowly read the parable of the Good Samaritan in Luke 10. Read it in at least five different Bible versions or translations in order to hear differing nuances. Meditate on some of the points about this passage that have been highlighted and studied in this chapter.

Recognize your resources. Reflect on your own heart, soul, strength, and mind. Make a list of what you know and what you possess. What is in your heart and soul? What are you passionate about? Is it gardening? Woodwork? Teaching a musical instrument? Maybe you love classic novels or jigsaw puzzles. What are you good at—your strength, talent, or skill? What do you know about? Maybe you are a history buff, or have a good knowledge about beekeeping, or the history of your neighborhood or city. Begin making a list that will help you to serve others and provide an example for your neighbors as they consider their own resources.

Consider others. Think about your neighbors. Who might be interested in joining you in making your neighborhood the best it has ever been? Begin with two categories: (1) Whom do you know the best? Whether you have lived there for a long time or briefly, whom are you closest to? (2) Whom have you spoken with, exchanged hellos with, or casually visited on the sidewalk or at the mailbox stand?

Pray. Begin praying for your neighborhood each day. Pray for the neighbors you know by name, as well as for those you know only by description. Pray for those you have never met. Pray for your neighborhood as a whole, that it becomes a place that experiences the peace and blessings of the Lord and the revelation of the gospel of the kingdom of heaven.

- 3 -

Your Community Bank

REALIZING OUR RESOURCES AND POSSIBILITIES

We are a community.
We are not ourselves by ourselves.
We are born into communities,
We live in communities, we die in communities.
Human beings are not solitary, self-sufficient creatures.

EUGENE PETERSON,
CHRIST PLAYS IN TEN THOUSAND PLACES

The essential challenge is to transform the isolation and self-interest
within our communities into connectedness and caring for the whole.
The key is to identify how this transformation occurs. We begin
by shifting our attention from the problems of community
to the possibility of community.

PETER BLOCK, *COMMUNITY*

HOW MUCH DO YOU HAVE IN THE BANK? No, not *that* bank. We're talking about your local *social* bank account. You may not even realize you have one. But think of it this way: If you were to look at all of your relationships—including the cumulative knowledge, wisdom, skills, talent, and shareable resources—you have among the people in your immediate neighborhood and community as an actual bank account, what shape is your account in? Is it well tended or overdrawn? If you needed to do so, could you write a check, or would it bounce?

Many people live within a few feet of people, or interact daily with the same folks repeatedly in the marketplace. But if they needed help, they would be unable to draw from this relational bank account. They are even at a loss as to how to make a *deposit* into this social bank account.

There is good news though. The assets in most neighborhoods are not running low. The problem is that we are mired in an inability to tap into these treasures. We have forgotten our access code. We simply need to recover it.

Few people give much thought to this type of community bank. When we need a product, solution, or service, our first thought is usually not *Whom do I know around me who has one of those, or who can help me with this or that?* Instead, we wonder where we can *buy* help: *Whom can I hire to do this for me?* It's really sad that Home Depot has a viable venture in renting out pickup trucks at an hourly rate. This is a sign of the relational bankruptcy going on in our culture: people have to go to a business and pay to use a truck, simply because they don't have someone nearby that could loan them one. It fails to occur to us that someone on our very street, or even a block or two over, has the capacity and even willingness to help or teach us how to help ourselves. Our relational network is down.

Consider your own ability—the things you know and have—that you, right now, are very much willing to share with others. We would be pleasantly surprised to discover the collective skills, wisdom, knowledge, tools, and keenness to share right under our noses. The problem is that few neighborhoods have the relational streams flowing that cause all this good stuff, life-making stuff to get passed around. Our concession to privacy and seclusion has served to dam up the very reserves of life-giving resources pooled around us.

No Home Is an Island

In recent years sociologists coined the term *social capital* to measure the degree to which people are connected in social networks, along with the overall value of those relationships. Author David Halpern defines the expression:

> Most people are embedded in a series of different social networks and associations. We have friends. We go to work and mix with colleagues. We may belong to a union or professional association that keeps us in touch with similar professionals outside of our own work context. In our leisure time, we may play a sport with a particular group or club, and we may belong to other interest-based groups, whether this interest is knitting, model railways or astrophysics. We may also belong to a political party, or more frequently, to a pressure group working to save whales, the environment, or the right to carry weapons. And in our home life, we are part of a family, a neighbourhood, and probably a religious

or ethnic community too. These everyday networks, including many of the social customs and bonds that define them and keep them together, are what we mean when we talk about social capital.[1]

Roughly two centuries ago, the French sociologist Alexis de Tocqueville penned *Democracy in America*, in which he praised the strength of the individual in American society. Yet simultaneously he issued a dire warning: This selfsame potency could mutate into a crippling weakness. The combination of individualism, addiction to privacy, and a consumerist mind-set can become a vault, locking away resources and functionality that are essential for a typical community to operate freely and fruitfully on its own.

Tocqueville proved to be prophetic. Think about it. When was the last time a neighbor knocked on your door to borrow an egg or cup of sugar? Whom do you know on your street who not only can play a musical instrument or fix cars but would be more than happy to teach the skill to others? Do you have relationships with wise elders in your neighborhood who can provide a listening ear and possibly sound advice? Maybe you are one of those elders; are there young couples around you who are taking advantage of your counsel or your good listening ear?

In the sharing of talents, experience, tools, libraries, appliances, relief, and care, relationships in a neighborhood and community are woven together, creating a fabric of social health surpassing the capacity and competency of any professional service industry, therapist, or caregiver. But this is far from the lived experience of most Westerners. We are a consumer society, and as such we are system-dependent. "We expect the school, coaches, agencies, and sitters to raise our children. . . . We expect doctors to keep us healthy. . . . We want social workers and institutions to take care of the vulnerable."[2] We have trouble imagining anything else. Authors John McKnight and Peter Block suggest that "in a consumer society, these functions are removed from family and community and provided by the marketplace; they are designed to be purchased."[3]

Happily, this is not everyone's experience. I (Lance) remember my sister's first car, a Chevrolet Vega, which she paid for by working at Dairy Queen. Besides being a product of the sorriest workmanship era in American car-manufacturing history, the little rattletrap of a car did not have an automatic transmission. My dad worked the night shift and wasn't able to teach my sister how to drive a stick shift, and my mom was too frightened to do it. But Jenny from across the street was more than happy to teach her. Jenny was in her late twenties; she listened to the same music as my sister. It was natural for my sister to look up to her and receive her advice. The time my sister spent with Jenny learning to drive set the table for Jenny to be able to speak into her life in a significant crisis. My sister had gotten to know and trust Jenny, who had experienced similar troubles in her own teen years. Jenny was able to understand and reach my sister in a way my mother could not.

Institutions, therapists, and professional trades and systems have their place. They are vital cogs on many levels of life.

But on their best days they cannot do many of the things that can only be done through relationships between humans who live near one another. Institutions can't be there for you on a moment's notice. They are not free. They lack the homespun touch. I remember neighborhood men teaching me about fishing, how to care for my hunting guns, how to change the oil in my car, how to spiral a football when you punt it, and how to spit tobacco juice farther than any of my buddies could.

In his bestselling book *Bowling Alone*, Robert Putnam underscored the importance of social capital for making a community thrive and be livable. In his own book on community building, Peter Block cites Putnam's discoveries:

> As one part of his extensive research, he studied a fair number of Italian towns and tried to understand why some were more democratic, were more economically successful, had better health, and experienced better education achievement. . . .
>
> He discovered that the one thing that distinguished the more successful from the less successful towns was the extent of social capital, or widespread relatedness that existed among its citizens. . . .
>
> Geography, history, great leadership, fine programs, economic advantage, and any other factors that we traditionally use to explain success made a marginal difference in the health of a community. Community well-being simply had to

do with the quality of the relationships, the cohesion that exists among its citizens.[4]

Most neighborhoods could legitimately be called *shelter-hoods*. Performing primarily as housing enclaves, they function as a collection of unconnected people. A smile while driving through, a "how ya doin'" while taking the trash to the curb, or a nod and a wave to the neighbor across the street is the depth of relationship most neighbors experience.

The downside of the "rugged individualism" Tocqueville pointed to germinated in the seedbeds of consumerism and privacy during the second half of the twentieth century. Marketers hyped what eventually became known as the "American dream" as the ultimate right and goal of life. But at what price? Increasingly we were raised to declare our independence from the people around us, to proclaim our emancipation from our neighbors and neighborhood. Our homes became our castles, our fences became our moats; our gates opened only from the inside. Though we are touted as the richest country in the world, the United States is statistically the most medicated nation as well.[5] The fact that these two notable data go hand in hand should cause us to ask some serious questions about the way we have come to do life.

How We Got Here

Immediately following World War II, a flood of returning armed servicemen reentered a recovered and now-bustling

American economy. These young, married men and their wives were in need of housing. Voila! The modern suburbs were born. Vast numbers of houses began to spring up at the edges of cities. American neighboring would quickly be changed, and not necessarily for the better.

A well-intentioned ruling by the Supreme Court in 1926 served to create what is perhaps the most hollowing aspect of typical contemporary American suburbia. The town of Euclid, Ohio, won the right to bar the development of land slated for an industrial-use complex. This was to protect the homes of nearby families from being fouled by factories and their toxic pollutants. Author Leigh Gallagher expounds:

> But it also made it constitutional for the first time for municipalities to separate the use of their land into buckets, designating certain areas for residential use, others for commerce, and others for industrial purposes. Later, when the FHA required single-use zoning as a condition for granting mortgages, this separation became baked into most new developments. More than almost anything else, single-use zoning permanently altered the look, feel, and overall DNA of our modern suburbs. Even now, single-use zoning is the easiest way to distinguish modern suburbs from their older counterparts. Instead of having a single downtown core with stores, apartments, and offices mixed together in one place, postwar suburbs typically separate everything:

subdivisions are off in one area, stores in another, and office space and industrial spaces in others.[6]

Though Euclidean zoning came into existence in 1926, it wasn't used widely prior to the post–World War II housing boom. The home I (Lance) live in was built in 1920. It sits in a suburb that typifies prewar suburbia. Sidewalks line both sides of the streets. Most houses have sitting porches facing the sidewalks. Several restaurants, pubs, coffee shops, and non–chain stores are within walking distance. It is not unusual each week for our car to be unused for a few days at a time.

Mixed-use zoning naturally fosters and encourages interaction among the residents of a neighborhood. My wife and I greet the same neighbors several times each week. They (or we) may be sitting on the front porch as we (or they) stroll by on the way to or from the coffee shop or pub, or while walking the dog. We run into these same neighbors in the places of business we frequent. It is normal to invite others for a dinner party or impromptu get-together. The ice is already broken between us.

Car Dependency

Contrast the dynamic of what have come to be dubbed as *walkable neighborhoods* with modern suburbs, largely designed using an abandonment of the urban-grid pattern found in older cities and neighborhoods. Most suburbs built over the last four or five decades favor "a circular, asymmetrical system made of curving subdivisions, looping streets, and cul-de-sacs."[7] They are car-necessary. Lance wrote about this in his book, *Right Here, Right Now*:

> The newer suburbs combine zoning ordinances with cul-de-sacs to minimize unnecessary traffic, making for quieter and safer living. Parents feel pretty secure in letting their children play in the cul-de-sac, as vehicular, drive-past traffic is minimal, and most of the cars that do come through are carrying residents of that street. . . .
>
> In the modern suburb there is no neighborhood Starbucks or drugstore. Marketplace activity is funneled to shopping centers and malls. Grocery stores, banks, drugstores, coffee shops, pubs, and schools are located *outside* of the neighborhood. This means people don't drive *through* on their way to another place or cross through as a short cut for other destinations. For the most part the people who drive there live there.[8]

A swelling commuter culture propelled by zoning laws, and the fact that most housing built in the last few decades is located a significant distance from the workplace, means we spend more time traveling farther and farther to get where we need to get. Consider that overall miles traveled per household annually increased 60 percent from 1969 to 2009. Leigh Gallagher writes, "The traditional American Dream said nothing about ninety-minute one-way commutes, but that's what people were willing to do to get the biggest, best home they could buy. By 2009 three million Americans were making 'extreme commutes' of three hours or more round-trip every weekday."[9]

Consider this in light of Putnam's research, which found that every ten minutes of commuting results in 10 percent fewer social connections.[10] In *Bowling Alone* Putnam emphasizes that single-use zoning results in people living their lives in large triangles, with stopping points where we sleep, work, and shop. A significant amount of our "free time" is spent going back and forth between these points. We might illustrate Putnam's research using the following graphic:

Just ask the typical suburban soccer mom what she spends the most time doing. You will likely be met with a sigh and a description of shuttling back and forth from home to work, schools, gyms, sports complexes, and the grocery store or fast food restaurant before going home in the evening. For churchgoers, top it off with attempts at connecting in a small group or regular church activities, and it is not hard to see that making time to connect with neighbors sounds like one more task to add to an already stressed-out life.

Income-Based and Single-Family Housing

One noticeable difference in older neighborhoods, in contrast to newer neighborhoods, is diversity in the size of homes. In older neighborhoods it is not unusual for a large (even stately) home to sit next door to a smaller-scaled home. Apartment buildings or multi-unit houses are home to singles and married folks alike. The various offerings of housing, in both scale and affordability, makes for a wide diversity among neighbors. The mixing of backgrounds, needs, wants, dreams, and assets—what each neighbor has to offer—is unique to each neighborhood and can be beautifully creative.

In an ever-increasing politically, racially, religiously, and socially divided America, we are in desperate need for people of different ages, ethnic and economic backgrounds, and even opinions to mingle and get to know one another. We don't understand people different from ourselves largely because we have become cordoned off into tight circles of sameness, packed with already-formed theories, beliefs, and emotionally charged opinions of what is wrong with "those people."

We would be quite remiss if we failed to acknowledge the racial divisions that continue to divide America, fostered at least in part by housing ordinances and codes written into the covenants of prewar suburbia. For example, the idyllic Brookside neighborhood within the Country Club District in Kansas City, where Lance lives, hides a sinister past. Blacks were not allowed to purchase homes in the housing development when it broke ground in 1920. Unimaginably, written covenants forbidding blacks from owning homes in some of the neighborhoods within this development remained in effect as late as 1992! This practice of "redlining" certain ethnicities from particular neighborhoods factored into the policies of the Home Owner's Loan Corporation, created during the New Deal in the wake of the Great Depression. "The result," writes Leigh Gallagher, "was a federal policy directing all money away from older urban neighborhoods and toward the suburbs, while at the same time effectively denying federal benefits to blacks that were flowing to whites."[11]

Premiums on Self-Sufficiency and Privacy

A society immersed in a vat of boiling individualism is the perfect mark for vendors of goods and services. Think back to Brad's reflections on the movie *Avalon*: A multigenerational family lived together, sharing one stove, one washing machine, one radio, one lawnmower, and so on.

If manufacturers could sell the American public on the idea that a more satisfying life—the "American dream"—consists of having your own this and that, then they could sell more this-and-thats. Rather than selling one radio, oven, or Sears kit house, they could sell two, three, or four.

In the boom years following World War II, dollars spent on food rose by 33 percent, and spending on clothes rose by 20 percent. Meanwhile, purchases of household furnishings and appliances surged by *240 percent*. In her book *The Way We Never Were*, author Stephanie Coontz writes, "Nearly the entire increase in the gross national product in the mid-1950s was due to increased spending on consumer durables and residential construction."[12]

With television, a match was made in corporate heaven. The producers of household products became the key sponsors of idyllic shows based on picture-perfect single-family households, including the earliest examples of product placement. The airwaves were filled with families living out the American dream: the Nelsons (*Ozzie and Harriet*), the Cleavers (*Leave It to Beaver*), the Andersons (*Father Knows Best*), the Ricardos (*I Love Lucy*), and many more. Elaine Tyler May writes:

> The legendary family of the 1950s . . . was not,
> as common wisdom tells us, the last gasp of
> "traditional" family life with deep roots in the past.
> Rather, it was the first wholehearted effort to create
> a home that would fulfill virtually all its members'

personal needs through an energized and expressive personal life.[13]

Besides the shows about white-picket-fenced-in nuclear families, the most popular shows on television in the 1950s were westerns, galvanized with a rugged, individualistic, make-it-on-your-own mindset. Not infrequently on shows such as *Bonanza* or *Wagon Train*, a family would find themselves in circumstances of lack or need. They would be offered help by townsfolk or a neighboring family, only to refuse the offer. "We don't take charity" was a socially admired declaration of self-sufficiency at all cost. Those who could not make it on their own experienced shame. Old-West historians will be quick to smirk at such notions, of course: Early American pioneers were greatly dependent upon government land grants and subsidies, as well as on one another, for survival and any hope of flourishing. If they didn't "take charity," they would eventually be pushing up daisies.

Individualism lies deep within the psyche of the typical American. Still, the degree of individualism that has become a source of national pride is actually a relatively recent phenomenon. As recently as 1938, Lewis Mumford critiqued the then-new suburbs as "a collective effort to live a private life." The surge in single-family home ownership between 1946 and 1956 exceeded the increase during the previous 150 years combined. In 1940 only 43 percent of American families owned their own homes. By 1960 the numbers had increased to 62 percent.

Philosophically speaking, individualism is very much the new kid on the block. Take Plato off the shelf and you will find he takes it for granted that the individual's place and purpose are defined by society, much as the place and purpose of the branch are defined by the tree. The idea that in essence the individual is complete on his own—that the tree does not exist until the branches agree to create it—appeared for the first time in post-Reformation Europe and remains, from the historical point of view, an enigma.[14]

Container Lifestyles

The factors we have viewed so far are part and parcel of the disjointedness most of us experience in our current neighborhoods. Our day-to-day living is carried out in de-integrated silos or containers. A variety of containers serve as holding places for commerce, employment, worship, exercise, education, and so forth. And rarely are these containers within our neighborhoods. Our neighborhoods function, in fact, as just one of these many containers—holding places for our sleeping and eating.

So our lives are spent scurrying about from one container to another. And the people frequenting these containers are usually not the same set of folks. The people we see at our favorite coffee shop are not the people we see at our gym. Our fitness friends are not our neighbors, and they don't know our neighbors. And our workplace friends don't know any of our coffee shop friends. Author Simon Carey Holt reflects on the container lifestyle dynamic:

> In truth, we spend as much time leaving the local neighborhood as we do living in it. The daily needs and opportunities to do so abound. It's most likely we will shop, work, worship and recreate in four entirely different spaces, with most of them well outside our neighborhoods.
>
> Similarly, when it comes to community, we'll draw on a network of relationships from multiple places. Indeed, so distinct are those places that it's rare for those we work with to have any significant connection to our family circle, or those with whom we worship, recreate or study. They may all inhabit the same city, but we'll interact with each community in different places. Cementing this change is the advent of the Internet and emails. Indeed, it's now likely that we'll communicate more often with someone interstate or overseas, than with the person next door.[15]

This dynamic makes it extremely difficult to have any notion of genuinely functioning community. It's hard to integrate such a wide variety of relationships from so many differing compartments. Life becomes a churning machine, made up of many parts, rather than an organic, holistic body of life.[16]

Our church container is no different. Unless we live in a smaller town, the people we worship with likely are from an altogether different container than those in our other life stations. With little to no naturally developed social capital to draw on (and most Christians giving little to no thought to their role in bringing the Good News of the kingdom of heaven to bear tangibly in their neighborhoods) even the most devoted church member's greatest hope for their nonbelieving acquaintances is to somehow persuade them to visit their church, there to be wooed or wowed by the worship team, sermon, or children's ministry that fills up their church container.

A prominent evangelical leader recently tweeted, "The most important moment each week in the life of the Christian is the preaching event in the local church." Between the two of us, we have over fifty years of preaching experience—we have preached literally thousands of sermons. But we don't believe for a second that the most important moment each week is the weekly sermon. Such wrongheaded thinking as this keeps the everyday Christian off the playing field. It keeps Christians from seeing their calling as missionaries to their neighborhoods as being every bit as high of a calling as the calling to preach in a pulpit. We are convinced that Jesus' message is not merely the *only* solution to life but a wonderfully beautiful solution. But Jesus' message must not be contained; it must break free from the confines of our church services. The imagination of the normal, everyday Christian must break out of the noncreative, blasé habits and expectations we have settled for. As Jon Shirley says, "You cannot change the city from the sanctuary. The fact that we thought we could means we missed the plot."[17]

Our role in weaving the social fabric of our neighborhoods is real and substantial in the eyes of God. It carries weight, and one can only imagine the impact across our cities if Christians were awakened to the meaningful transformation that can take place when we realize the budding potential we hold. Each Christian is called to be a restorer and reconciler:

> Therefore, if anyone is in Christ, he is a new creation. The old has passed away; behold, the new has come. All this is from God, who through Christ reconciled us to himself and gave us the ministry of reconciliation; that is, in Christ God was reconciling the world to himself, not counting their trespasses against them, and entrusting to us the message of reconciliation.
>
> 2 CORINTHIANS 5:17-19, ESV

As a Christian, you are *in Christ—in Jesus*. And God is in Jesus, still reconciling the world to himself. The apostle Paul says God has "entrusted" this message to us. That's pretty heavy stuff. God trusts you and me with his message of reconciliation. And just as Jesus did, this message doesn't get delivered merely in words. It gets delivered with words *and* deeds. It gets delivered by followers of Jesus who are willing to terminate the American dream where it gets in the way of heaven dispensing its goods in the neighborhood.

Reflection and Preparation

Conduct an audit of your neighborhood:

- To your knowledge, what notable skills or talents are held, and by whom, in your neighborhood?
- How far away is the closest coffee shop or pub to your house? Is it a walkable distance, or does it require a drive?
- How much time do you estimate you spend driving on an average weekday?
- Does the architecture of the houses in your neighborhood encourage privacy or neighborly interaction?
- What elements exist in your neighborhood that encourage interaction among neighbors (a neighborhood newsletter, Facebook group, associations, community garden, and so on)?
- How ethnically, economically, and generationally diverse is your neighborhood?
- How many local businesses are owned by people who live in your neighborhood?
- In what ways are new neighbors welcomed to your neighborhood?

- 4 -
Here Comes the Neighborhood

MOVING FROM SCARCITY TO ABUNDANCE

*Professionalization is the market replacement for a community
that has lost or outsourced its capacity to care.*

JOHN McKNIGHT AND PETER BLOCK,
THE ABUNDANT COMMUNITY

*True belonging is born of relationships not only to one another
but to a place of shared responsibilities and benefits. We love not so much
what we have acquired as what we have made and whom
we have made it with.*

ROBERT FINCH

AFTER SEVERAL YEARS serving as missionaries in Mexico, Kurt Rietema and his wife moved into an Argentine neighborhood in Kansas City, Kansas. It wasn't long before they began to experience the kindness and generosity of their Hispanic neighbors who rented the house next door. Not only did this family share food with other neighbors, they also voluntarily landscaped people's yards and watered their gardens. Kurt says, "All the grand illusions of my own generosity were shattered by living among Mexican immigrants who send half of their paychecks back home to their families in Mexico. And they're making way less than I am."

One afternoon Kurt was visiting Hector, the father of

the family. Kurt was disappointed to learn they were planning to move. Hector said they did not want to move from the neighborhood, but the continually escalating monthly expenses had become too much for them to afford. When Kurt discovered the amount they were paying each month in rent, he was dismayed. This family was being taken advantage of by an out-of-state behemoth that owned a multitude of houses across the country. His love for his neighbors and the blessing they were to the entire neighborhood would not let him stand pat.

Kurt asked whether Hector had considered buying the house. Hector said they had inquired about that a few years earlier, but the price was too high. When Hector told Kurt the asking price, he again was appalled. The amount was way beyond reason. He asked Hector whether he would like him to do some investigating on the possibility of them buying the house. Hector quickly said yes, thanking Kurt for helping out, even if it appeared to be a long shot.

Let's pause for a moment in this story and make some observations. For the most part, in North American culture, we are conditioned to think as citizens more so than neighbors. Neighbors are concerned with responsibility. Citizens are concerned with rights. Neighbors are concerned with accountability. Citizens are concerned with entitlement. When we live primarily from our citizenry, we lose the selflessness that comes from being a good and loving neighbor. But citizens who are also good neighbors are different. Peter Block writes:

The willingness to care for the whole . . . flows out
of the kind of conversations we have about the new
story we want to take our identity from. It means
we have conversations of what we can do to create
the future. Entitlement is a conversation about what
others can or need to do to create the future for us.[1]

Incompetent communities operate from a scarcity mentality. Particularly in the post–9/11 age, ours is a culture mar-
inated in fear, anxiety, distrust, anger, and suspicion. This
atmosphere is perfectly suited to turn us extremely inward,
to focus us tightly on self-protection. Neighborhoods that
lack the local and personal interaction, concern, and inter-
dependency characteristic of a neighboring mind-set breed a
scarcity mentality at a time when we need a mutuality mentality more than ever. Now that so many people live sizeable
distances away from extended family members, the natural
support systems provided by family are largely out of reach.
In their place, professional systems have taken over, to such
a point that most of us assume we lack the resources and
capacity to meet many of our day-to-day needs, let alone the
needs of our neighbors. This is what we are referring to when
we speak of a *scarcity mentality*.

Among evangelical Christians, the "me and mine first"
attitude that accompanies a scarcity mentality is contrary to
the gospel we say we believe in. The entitlement mentality of a citizen-consumer mindset, coupled with the insecu-
rity of a scarcity mentality, makes us averse to commitment

beyond our own four walls, outsourcing those commitments to the government and other large-scale entities. We become "addicted to accepting the illusion of safety that we get from allowing large systems to name the game and define the conversation."[2] But the essence of citizenship in the kingdom of heaven is captured in the words of Paul: "Let no one seek his own good, but the good of his neighbor" (1 Corinthians 10:24, ESV), and further, "Let each of you look not only to his own interests, but also to the interests of others." (Philippians 2:4, ESV).

This is what we are seeing in Kurt, as he takes time and energy to help his neighbor Hector:

> I talked to the property manager and told her I hated to see my neighbors have to move away and asked if she thought the owners might be willing to sell the house. She said, "Well, the house is owned by a big conglomerate down in Texas, and it is really just a line item on their spreadsheet." She asked me what I thought the house was worth. I threw out a figure that was slightly more than one-third the price that had been quoted to my neighbors. Just a few days later, the property manager called me and said, "The seller accepted your offer."[3]

I didn't make an offer, Kurt thought. But that was not how he responded to the agent. "Great, let's do it," he said.

Next up was to find financing for Hector and his family.

The logical (systems-focused) way would be to go to a big bank or mortgage loan corporation. And that was Kurt's first move. But after checking interest rates and the associated fees, Kurt wasn't satisfied. He was convinced there must be a better solution out there, somewhere.

Let's pause again. Unquestionably we are blessed by many wonderful people who have committed their lives to serving others in the settings of professional institutions and systems. Institutions are certainly needed. Not a day goes by that we are not served well by a multiplicity of institutions and professional service providers. But we get off-kilter when we live with the mentality that the first and best answer always comes from the professional realm. The subtitle of John McKnight and Peter Block's seminal book *The Abundant Community* is *Awakening the Power of Families and Neighborhoods*. Their thesis is that our communities—our neighborhoods—possess abundant resources and potential for problem solving and the meeting of needs. But rather than picking up the mantle of neighborliness, we have surrendered to *system* life. We pay professionals to deal with our problems and troubles—even a lot of normal life stuff. It doesn't occur to us to do anything else.

Here is the rub: Systems that are constructed for order cannot provide satisfaction in domains that require a unique and personal human solution. They are unable to provide the satisfaction that they promise because of their very nature. This is not a critique of any individual's leadership or method of operation. It is that systems have a limit; by their nature, they cannot provide prosperity or peace of mind or a life of satisfaction.[4]

As he considered his neighbor's situation, Kurt thought, *I've got a lot of friends in some area churches that are from the suburbs and would love to get involved and help out in some way in the urban corridor. I might be able to get a better rate for my neighbors and create a good investment opportunity for my friends.* In short order Kurt received replies from an e-mail he sent to a few friends. Several of them chipped in to make the home loan.

It was a win for everyone. Hector's family went from being renters to becoming homeowners, and their monthly payment was cut in half. Kurt's suburban friends were overjoyed that they could help out while getting a fair return on their investment. The experience worked out so well for everyone that several houses in Kurt's neighborhood have changed hands under similar terms. Kurt has taken seriously the call to make his neighborhood *livable*, a wonderful taste of heaven on earth.

Abundance-Thinking Neighborhoods

Shifting from a scarcity, system-bound mind-set to an abundant neighborhood mindset comes as we unleash the variety of gifts, talents, resources, wisdom, and imagination of our families and neighbors. We learn to inventory our collective resources, focusing on what we have rather than what we don't have. Our neighborhoods become competent communities when neighbors themselves shift from complacency to caring. We care for our neighbors as we care for ourselves.

Our first thought may be, *But not everyone is going to participate.* That is true. *Everyone* won't, but many will. While consumer society celebrates individualism—turning eyes and hearts inward—a commitment to faithfully stewarding our station in the history of our neighborhoods sparks a collective identity among the residents of our streets and communities.

We are certainly not trying to paint an unrealistic utopian portrait. But we are seeking to give vision to what can happen when heavenly minded people determine to do earthly good in the places they live, work, and play. An abundance-minded community operates from a different belief system than those functioning from the consumer, systems-bound default.

In the late 1980s, when I (Lance) discovered my wife was pregnant, we immediately made an appointment with a doctor and began learning all we needed to know to be prepared for having our first child. But we soon began to feel somewhat disillusioned and a bit apprehensive with the normal *baby-having* system. Everything felt so institutionalized and impersonal. We could not come to grips with strangers controlling one of the most important and personal moments of our lives. (This was almost thirty years ago; "birthing rooms," which provide a much more personal atmosphere, were virtually nonexistent at the time. It had just been a few years since the father was allowed in the delivery room.)

We found what we were looking for when we were introduced to a wonderful midwife. Her name was Helen, and we fell in love with her. To top it off, her last name was Jolly! A last name could not be more fitting for such a wonderful soul. Helen became a trusted friend and midwife who subsequently delivered all three of our children. Midwifery was quite unheard of at the time, and the blowback we (and our parents) received from friends were pretty hard-hitting. Many people questioned our sanity and, in some cases, disqualified us as good parents. For many people, the baby-having system was the only sensible or acceptable option—despite the majority of the world delivering children with the assistance of midwives.

This is the overload that systems dependency causes. At best it has provided an existence, but very little *abundant* life. McKnight and Block wrote about a friend who works with developmentally disabled people; most of the disabled individuals he worked with had few if any friends. The people who spend time with them are paid to do so.

Earthly minded citizenship looks to institutional powers to address the problems and ills of the day. This feeds a consumer mentality that often negates tangible actions at the local, next-door level. As Walter Brueggemann says, "Those who are living in anxiety and fear, most especially fear of scarcity, have no time or energy for the common good."[5] A scarcity mentality causes us to hold back the abundance God has blessed us with. It keeps us from seeing resources all around us, and it fosters hoarding and a preoccupation with security.

But Jesus never offered a safe walk. Crosses are anything but safe. We must be renewed by our true identity as Jesus people. We are not sent out just with words of hope for a future post-death life in heaven. Jesus commissions his followers to ditch anxieties linked to clothing, food, and shelter and to seek the manifestation of his kingdom and all it offers. His promise is to provide all our needs as he instructs us to abstain from hoarding earthly resources.

> Do not lay up for yourselves treasures on earth,
> where moth and rust destroy and where thieves
> break in and steal, but lay up for yourselves treasures
> in heaven, where neither moth nor rust destroys and
> where thieves do not break in and steal. For where
> your treasure is, there your heart will be also.
> MATTHEW 6:19-21, ESV

> Therefore do not be anxious, saying, "What shall we
> eat?" or "What shall we drink?" or "What shall we
> wear?" For the Gentiles seek after all these things,
> and your heavenly Father knows that you need
> them all. But seek first the kingdom of God and his
> righteousness, and all these things will be added to
> you.
> MATTHEW 6:31-33, ESV

Those who embrace their heavenly citizenship and allow the creativity of heaven to ebb and flow in their own minds become the best neighbors on earth. In contrast, when we are given over to the subtle undertones of a scarcity mentality, the very abundance we possess gets locked away—where, Jesus warns, it rots, decays, and disappears. It is mind-boggling to consider that the self-storage business in the United States is a 23 billion dollar industry—more profitable than the entertainment industry. It seems that Jesus could have had the storage industry in mind when he told the parable of the rich fool who was overrun with a fantastic harvest (Luke 12:16-21). He built bigger and bigger barns, telling himself that he could take it easy and gluttonize himself. Jesus goes on to say that God rebuked the rich man for storing up his treasures rather than being rich toward God.

In his book *Right Here, Right Now* (coauthored with Lance), Alan Hirsch commented on the dangers of unrestrained consumerism:

> The hidden danger of unbridled consumption is that in the end we are the ones being consumed. Our freedom for true joy and our ability to live out our God-given calling as agents of the King is swallowed up and entangled in the web of consumption. But when we are freed from the love and greedy acquisition of more things, we are liberated to be generous transmitters of Jesus' phenomenal grace and kindness. This yields a real and lasting fulfillment that leaves the consumerist pursuit of happiness in the dust.[6]

The Roseto Effect

In the early 1960s a happenstance conversation over beers one evening between two doctors was the precursor to what has come to be known as "the Roseto effect." A local physician casually mentioned to the head of medicine at the University of Oklahoma that it seemed as if heart disease was rarer in his town of Roseto, a small village nestled in the hills of eastern Pennsylvania named for the Italian city that are the roots of its founders, in comparison to nearby cities. Researchers began an extensive study of Roseto, discovering a near-zero cardiac mortality rate for men aged fifty-five to sixty-four. For men above sixty-five, the local death rate was half the national average.[7]

Why did this diminutive Italian-immigrant settlement boast such extraordinary heart health? Researchers assumed the answer lay in diet, exercise, and labor habits. But the investigators were stunned to discover this was not the case at all. The citizens drank plenty of wine and subsisted on classic Italian foods rich with cholesterol-laden pastas and sausages deep-fried in animal fat. Smoking was a daily habit for the men, who worked in back-breaking and toxic conditions in the local quarry.

None of this made sense to the researchers. The medical field was stumped. Microscopes would not be able to solve the mystery. So they brought in clipboard-carrying sociologists, who visited with town officials and went door to door to interview the Roseto citizens. Several unusual elements caught the eye of the researchers. For starters, the crime rate was zero, and there were no applications for public assistance. Yes, you read that right: no crime and no social services requested. Nada. Zilch. A rich community-wide social life was practiced, not divided along economic or educational lines. The haves and have-nots played, partied, and prayed together. The wealthy did not flaunt their affluence and seemed to make a conscious effort to avoid doing so. Local businesses received virtually all patronage of the townsfolk, despite larger stores nearby in surrounding towns. And though families were close-knit and took special care of their own, researchers discovered a spirit of assistance, friendly concern, and a tangible regard for neighbors and non-family as well.

It seemed to the examiners that no one was alone. The elderly were not placed into institutions and were actually "installed as informal judges and arbitrators in everyday life and commerce."[8]

The medical community was left to conclude that the secret of such astonishingly high cardiac health in individuals in Roseto was because of the community heart that beat for one another. The people in the community had healthy hearts because the community had a heart for one another.

Sadly, the Roseto effect would not last. In 1963 researchers keenly predicted that "as Rosetans became more Americanized (meaning less close, less modest and less interdependent), they would also become less healthy."[9] The *American Journal of Public Health* revisited Roseto in 1992 and found Rosetans suffering the same statistical rate of heart disease as neighboring cities. What happened? Single-family homes had become the new norm, fences appeared, and churches moved to the outskirts of town. Community fabric wore thin, and with it the sheltering warmth it had provided.

The lessons from Roseto are remarkable. Roseto had been a competent community. While its inhabitants were no wealthier than the average American town, their quality of life was improved by their interconnectedness. Abundant communities have the capacity to take care of one another. They are convinced the basic everyday needs, along with many unexpected bumps in the road of life, can be met by the collective talent, skill, wisdom, and durable goods already present in the homes and garages in their neighborhoods.

Relational Rhythms

In *The R Factor*, authors Michael Schluter and David Lee refer to "relational proximity" as a shaping factor of how functional our community connections are. This is not the same as geographical proximity. People can live next door to one another or work in the same office with one another for years, yet not know each other in any meaningful way.[10] Certain factors or dimensions determine the level of relational proximity that exists between individuals. Some of them are particularly relevant to better neighboring.

Directness: proximity in contact. This has to do with actual face-to-face time—real, up-close physical presence with one another. Seeing someone across the driveway or backyard fence falls short of this type of directness (as does FaceTime on your iPhone).

The movie *The Sandlot* relates the tale of a group of scrappy young boys in the early 1960s. They spend their summer days playing baseball on a patchwork neighborhood field. Beyond the outfield fence is "the Beast," an elephant-sized dog whose mouth makes baseballs look like golf balls. The legend of the terror dog and his mean-spirited master holds the boys in fear all summer long. After a rare collector ball accidentally gets put into play and ends up in the mouth of the Beast, however, the boys are forced to knock on the door of the owner's house in an attempt to recover it. Once the boys meet and enter the home of the dog's owner, a transformation takes place: The Beast shrinks to a normal-sized, playful English mastiff, and the cruel master becomes a smiling, gregarious man who helps the boys out of a jam. The dog didn't literally shrink, of course, and the old man didn't suddenly become kind. Any transformation that took place did so in the minds of the boys. Once they slowed down and connected with the dog and his owner, everything changed.

Directness transforms relationships because it changes perceptions and our understanding of one another. When we fail to enter into the dimension of directness, we continue to base our perception of others on our preconceived notions and myths.

Continuity: proximity through time. Abundant neighborhoods have people who set aside time for one another. They are convinced that a satisfied life is impossible apart from authentic relationships and frequent interaction among neighbors. Therefore, they believe to neglect time for their neighbors is to miss out on an essential part of living itself.

Just as geographical proximity is not enough to foster meaningful relationships, the mere passage of time does not make relationships grow either. We need regular contact with people to cultivate and sustain bonds. Just think back to your closest friends in high school, or take a look back at your wedding photographs. When was the last time you spoke with or hung out with those people? People we once considered to be our best friends quite often are folks we have not had contact with in years.

If not for Facebook we would not know where many of the people with whom we once were like "peas in a pod" even live now. I (Lance) recently asked my daughter, married just five years ago, how one of her bridesmaids was doing. "Huh," she said. "I don't know. I haven't seen her in years." These close friends had not had an argument or blowup. As each of their lives evolved, they simply drifted apart. It takes continuity to keep relationships alive.

Multiplexity: proximity in multiple spheres. Several years ago, while living in a small Missouri town, I (Lance) purchased a couple of bicycles from a small bike shop. The guy who ran the place was doing some adjustments to the brakes and gears on the bikes before I took them home. I stood by while he rode one of the bikes down the street to check his adjustments. His little four-year-old girl was standing next to me with a lollipop in her mouth, watching her dad. I said, "Your dad is the bike man, isn't he?" She pulled the sucker out of her mouth with a loud pop and glared at me. Jutting her chin out, she shouted, "He's Daddy Man!" I had been thoroughly rebuked. In three words that little girl let me know that my edited version of her dad would not be tolerated in her presence.

Many of our community relationships are limited because we box people into an identity defined by their vocational role. We characterize people with what we see them *do*: the mailman, the FedEx guy, the dry-cleaning lady, and so on. To only relate to a person in the sphere of what they do will not build an actual relationship. It will fail to see them as they really are—a whole person made in the image of God.

No too long ago one of our buddies started a weekly gathering of guys around a fire pit in his front yard. With no planned studies or curriculum, they just talk about life and what God has to say about that. One day our friend received a package delivery from UPS. He had made small talk with the delivery driver over the years, but that was as far as it went. When the UPS guy glanced over at the fire pit, complimenting it, our buddy felt the Holy Spirit urge him to tell the guy what it was for and to invite him to join the next gathering. The UPS guy immediately accepted, telling our friend that he really needed something like that in his life.

Not surprisingly, the UPS guy is not known as the "UPS guy" anymore. He has become Brian—friend guy. As the relationship progressed, our pal and Brian have gotten to know each other in multiple spheres: as fire-pit mates, husbands, and fathers.

Commonality: proximity of purpose. My (Lance's) mother lived through the World War II years and has shared many stories of her tight-knit little hometown and the interconnectedness of the wider American community during the war years. The rationing of gas, chocolate, sugar—just about everything but water—was rarely met with complaint. Rather, it was seen as a way to participate in victory by those who were enlisted as armed forces service men or women. Things changed quickly when the war was over, however. Although it was obviously a good thing that Americans were not speaking German in 1946, the commonality of the previous five years quickly gave way to individualism and the attitudes and postures of consumerism. My mom has always felt a sadness in that thought.

Abundance-thinking neighbors value stewardship over ownership. They believe their homes are not just for themselves, and their resources—vehicles, tools, books, entertainment media, and the like—are placed in their care to be enjoyed and shared with others. My father-in-law is seventy-seven years old. He retired to Florida from his orthodontic practice in a small Missouri town several years ago. Over the last couple of years, he and my wife's mother began thinking deeper about their role in their adopted city. They took notice of the needs of some of their neighbors, as well as various individuals and families in their church. As I write this he is putting the finishing touches on a massive project—a commercial-sized greenhouse system, which he has built himself through hours and hours of hard, sweaty work and no small amount of cash. Through a system called aquaponics he will be raising enormous amounts of fresh vegetables and fish to provide food for his family, his neighbors, and friends from his church. He is in the stage of life where he has "earned the right" to kick back and dig his toes into the sandy beaches. He has chosen to bring good news to his neighborhood instead. He values his call as a citizen of the kingdom of heaven, which requires him to live his life as a faithful neighbor on earth.

The course my father-in-law has chosen for his final chapter of life reminds me of these words from the apostle Paul:

> There are many out there taking other paths,
> choosing other goals, and trying to get you to go
> along with them. I've warned you of them many
> times; sadly, I'm having to do it again. All they want
> is easy street. They hate Christ's Cross. But easy
> street is a dead-end street. Those who live there make
> their bellies their gods; belches are their praise; all
> they can think of is their appetites.
>
> But there's far more to life for us. We're citizens of
> high heaven!
>
> PHILIPPIANS 3:18-20, MSG

When neighbors join in on projects such as a community garden, block parties, neighborhood garage sales, or political referendums, they come close to one another. The purpose makes them one people—at least more so than they were beforehand. Let us, then, determine to bring abundance to our neighborhoods. These are the stations of our assignment as citizens of the kingdom of heaven. As heavenly people, stationed in our neighborhood or apartment complex, let's do our part to eliminate the scarcity mentality that grips our consumer culture and help next door taste a bit of heaven.

Reflection and Preparation

Consider the following questions:

- To what degree has a scarcity mentality found a place in your thinking?
- How do you see yourself in regard to "systems" dependency?
- To what degree is your neighborhood abundance-minded? Do you see much thought and action given to "one another"?

Consider sitting down with your family and creating a neighborhood declaration of interdependence. See the example on the next page:

Our Neighborhood Declaration of Interdependence

We, the Christians of the _____
neighborhood, in order to form a more perfect
community, provide for the common good,
ensure tranquility, and share in the joy of our own
individual blessings,

- believe God has sent us to our neighborhood;
- believe God has gifted us to share our stuff with our
  neighbors;
- believe there are gifts for us to receive from others;
- trust the gifts are present to make a better
  neighborhood;
- hold ourselves accountable for the welfare of our
  neighborhood;
- choose to steward our gifts and power rather than
  be passive or possessive, or to leave it to others to fix
  what is broken; and
- choose to become active in excavating and activating
  the gifts of others.

- 5 -

Getting to Know You

SEEING YOUR NEIGHBORS FOR WHO THEY REALLY ARE

I don't see crowds, I see individuals.

MOTHER TERESA

I wonder how many people I've looked at all my life and never seen.

JOHN STEINBECK, *THE WINTER OF OUR DISCONTENT*

IN THE STREETS of a desperate and hopeless Calcutta, the little nun known as Mother Teresa worked for six decades. She said the secret to not letting herself become overwhelmed by the masses in need was that she didn't see masses. She saw a person in the midst of masses.

Mother Teresa took her cues from Jesus. In the Gospels we see case after case of Jesus moving among the crowds and zeroing in on individuals, subsequently transforming their lives. Seeing a funeral procession, his eyes moved through the denseness of the mourners to settle upon the broken and weeping mother of a young boy being carried away for burial. On another occasion as he was surrounded by pressing crowds, his eyes focused on a man in a tree whom he knew needed an encounter with him. At yet another time his gaze zeroed in on one particular tax collector, one of the most despised professions in Jewish culture at the time. Jesus invited this man named Levi (later called Matthew) to follow him as a disciple.[1]

Bestselling author Peter Senge relates the customary greeting of a particular tribal people.

> Among the tribes of northern Natal in South Africa, the most common greeting, equivalent to "hello" in English, is the expression: *Sawu bona*. It literally means, "I see you." If you are a member of the tribe, you might reply by saying *Sikhona*, "I am here." The order of the exchange is important: until you see me, I do not exist. It's as if, when you see me, you bring me into existence.[2]

A deep truth resides in this cultural practice. When we merely move through our days without seeing people as *people*, then as far as it matters to us in that moment, they really don't exist. We are busy people, living in a busy world. Yet, we are called by the Lord to bring out the "God-flavors" to the places we carry out our lives (Matthew 5:13, MSG)—salting the earth with joy, kindness, smiles, laughter, and more. Being conscious of how we approach people we encounter through the normal routines of our day is a step toward bringing out the tastes of heaven here on our patch of earth.

Although Jesus said it in the midst of his most famous sermon, few of us have taken seriously his probing question: "If you greet only your brothers, what more are you doing than others? Do not even the Gentiles do the same?" (Matthew 5:47, ESV). The word *greet* in the original Greek means to receive joyfully, to welcome, to draw to one's self. This is incredibly practical stuff Jesus is emphasizing. He is saying, "Don't be like people who don't have the Holy Spirit in them. Be different—not by your bumper stickers and Facebook memes, but on the streets, in your workplace, and in the marketplace, in the way you wish others well and receive others with delight."

Knowing You Knowing Me

A few years ago I (Lance) had the opportunity to meet one-on-one with my childhood hero, Roger Staubach—the greatest quarterback of the greatest team (the Dallas Cowboys) in the history of the greatest sport in all of ever (American football). He's not just my childhood hero. He is my adulthood hero. I had met Roger four decades earlier, following a freak accident that left me with a life-threatening head injury. In 2012, on a whim, I sent an email to his company with a newspaper article and picture from our meeting in 1972. Within hours his assistant emailed me back. Three weeks later I sat alone in an elaborate, glass-walled conference room overlooking the scenic downtown Dallas skyline, waiting on Roger to arrive. As he walked into the room, a big smile crossed his face as he said, "Hi Lance!" What? He didn't say, "Hi there," or "Hey fella." No. Wow! *He knows my name*, I thought. *Roger Staubach just called me by my name! I'm not washing the inside of my ears for months. I don't want to wash the sound of that out.* I didn't feel like just another of the millions of Roger Staubach fans. I was *Lance Ford*, friend of Roger Staubach. I was going to need to get new business cards.

Now, the reality is that Roger gets lots of requests, and he meets and greets thousands of fans. His secretary probably had the article lying on his desk right before he walked in. "Okay, this guy's name is Lance . . . Lance . . . Lance . . ." Roger probably recited to himself just before entering the room. Doesn't matter to me. All I know is Roger Staubach came in and greeted me by name, and we visited for about half an hour alone before he signed a football with "Your friend, Roger Staubach" at the end.

What happens in your heart when you come across someone you have not seen in a while? If that person greets you with "Hi there" or "Hey gal," that is one thing. But if they use your name, it is an altogether different feeling. You feel like an actual somebody, not just another *anybody*. You feel more complete in the eyes of the other person. You come into being at another level.

When Jay Pathak and Dave Runyon joined with a group of fellow Denver-area pastors to discuss ways to lead their congregations into better practices of neighboring, they ended up creating a simple tool that has become tremendously helpful as a metric for how well we know our neighbors. Imagine a tic-tac-toe grid. There are nine boxes. The middle box represents your house and the surrounding eight boxes represent your neighbors' homes.

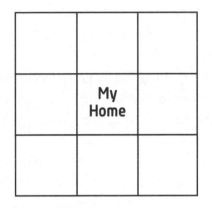

The challenge is to see how many neighbors' names you can fit in each box. For instance, the boxes above and below the "My Home" box represent the homes directly behind and in front of yours; the boxes to each side represent the homes next door to yours.

Jay and Dave have told us that in a typical audience they present to, only about 10 percent of people can fill in the names for all eight boxes. We have used this tool dozens of times ourselves and have found similar results.

Jesus says that the second-most important command-ment—on which all the others hang—revolves around good, loving neighboring:

You shall love the Lord your God with all your heart
and with all your soul and with all your mind. This
is the great and first commandment. And a second is
like it: You shall love your neighbor as yourself. On
these two commandments depend all the Law and
the Prophets.

MATTHEW 22:37-40, ESV

Loving our actual neighbors begins with actually knowing them. And knowing them starts with knowing their
names.

Many people live in apartment buildings or neighborhoods for years without ever knowing their neighbors' names,
much less anything significant about their lives. Consider the
following excerpt from a 2014 *Maclean's* article:

It's a new day in the neighborhood all across
the Western world. More than 30 percent of
Canadians now say they feel disconnected from
their neighbors, while half of Americans admit
they don't know the names of theirs. An Australian
sociologist investigating community responses in
the wake of the 2011 floods in Queensland found
relations in "a precarious balance"; neighbors were
hesitant to intrude even in emergencies—leading
the scholar to conclude that "we are less likely than
ever to know" our neighbors. Quite right, too: A
recent poll of 2,000 Britons found a third declaring

they couldn't pick their near neighbors out of a police lineup.[3]

Talk about going back to the starting line. Many of us will need to begin our mission of neighborliness with the simple step of getting to know the *names* of our neighbors. Only then can we begin to know something about their actual lives. This may mean we knock on our neighbors' doors with a plate of cookies and humbly say something along the lines of, "Hi, I'm from a couple doors down. I feel embarrassed that I don't know (or remember) your name, and I would really like to." Most likely, that neighbor will ditto your feeling, tell you so, and the ice will immediately be broken. Bam! You've made a huge leap toward getting to know a neighbor.

The Incarnation was not only the most humongous measure of God reaching out to broken humanity; it was also the most humble act. Jesus laid aside his rights and privileges. He went from every abundant thing that heaven had to offer to every hard thing that earth would demand. For us to humble ourselves via the slight embarrassment or unease that may come with introducing—or reintroducing—ourselves to those in the neighborhood we are digging into is a small price to pay in our attempts at following the ways of Jesus.

Most people move into a neighborhood with every desire and intention of getting to know their neighbors. Why does it not happen with more regularity? Because it doesn't just *happen*. We must make it happen.

The Image of God

Some of the most awe-inspiring moments of our lives are those times we find ourselves in the midst of God's creation. If you have stood at the edge of the Grand Canyon or on the shores of Sydney harbor or in the heart of Yellowstone, you know what we are talking about. Our hearts thrill at the wonder of a new-born baby horse, puppy, or baby chick. As I (Lance) write this I am looking out my upper library window at a squirrel, down below on the wooden fence, enjoying an apple core retrieved from our compost bin. Creation! Amazing and breathtaking.

As astounding as creation is, no part of it is as truly incredible as a human being. Every human being. The ones we love and like, but also the ones we loathe and despise. When our eyes come upon a human we are looking at the only part of creation that is made in the image of God himself. That is an amazing thought if we let it settle in.

To be in the presence of even the meanest, lowest, most repulsive specimen of humanity is still to be closer to God than when looking up into a starry sky or at a beautiful sunset. For we cannot really love a sunset; we can love only a person. God is love, and in coming to Him, we cannot escape coming through people. There is no separation between the spiritual and the social. The way we feel about people is the way we feel about God, and the way we treat people is the way we treat God.[4]

I love puppies. I don't like jerks. But jerks are still made in the image of God. Lassie isn't.

One time on an ocean cruise I (Lance) had an experience that has had a lasting effect on me for well over a decade since it happened. If you have ever been on a cruise, you know that photographers set up staging areas to take pictures of individuals and couples as they disembark for a port of call or before a special evening dinner. The pictures are later posted for passengers to look at and decide if they would like to purchase them.

On this particular evening, I finished sitting in on an art auction aboard the ship, and then went looking through the hundreds of photos on the wall, hunting for those of my family and me. The conversation in my mind was outright ugly. *Ouch, dude needs braces. Dang, buddy. That combover makes Donald Trump's hair look great. Lady, you really need to skip a couple or ten meals.* The comments in my head went on and on. Suddenly I was interrupted by the Lord's voice. "Why are you making fun of my artwork? This afternoon you *oohed* and *ahhed* over the work of men and women with oil and charcoal on canvas. Here you are looking at flesh and blood on the framework of the most splendidly functioning system imaginable. I have handmade billions of humans over the course of history, and there are not so much as two of them who are alike. I am the Master, and each one is a masterpiece. Would you like to see them as I see them?"

I was stunned. The voice of the Lord was that distinct. I said, "Yes, please." For the next twenty minutes I was overcome by the absolute beauty in each and every face in those pictures. The distinctness of every nose, eye, lip, hair, bald head, and big and small set of ears absolutely amazed me. Every person is a handmade art-image of God himself.

Jesus said that to give (or deny) a cup of cold water to someone who is thirsty, or to visit (or ignore) a prisoner, is to do the same to him. His point was that there is a piece of him in every single human being we come across. A lot of Christians like to post memes on Facebook that say something like, "Jesus says if you deny me before men then I will deny you before God." Supposedly, if you don't hit *share*, then you are denying Jesus. Poppycock! The same people who piously or fearfully pass on such ideas are often the same Christians who, by their treatment of other people, consistently deny and ignore Jesus.

How Jesus Saw

Most of us are familiar with the account of Jesus and the young man commonly known as the rich young ruler (Mark 10:17-25). This young man approached Jesus, asking him what was necessary for him to obtain eternal life. In the midst of Jesus' answer, the young guy (possibly interrupting Jesus) said he had kept the Ten Commandments since his childhood. It is possible—and I believe likely—that he was a bit arrogant with his reply; the text says he was trying to "justify himself."

At this point in the narrative, Mark writes, "Then Jesus *beholding him* loved him" (KJV, emphasis added). The Greek word for "beholding" speaks of the study of the constella-tions; it means something much deeper than to simply notice or glance at. Thayer's lexicon defines it:

Beholding
1. to have (the power of) understanding
2. to discern mentally, observe, perceive, discover, understand
3. to turn the thoughts or direct the mind to a thing, to consider, contemplate, to look at, to weigh carefully, examine[5]

To "behold" is to intensely consider or pay mind to some-thing or someone. The text doesn't say Jesus loved the young man and then beheld him. It flips the sequence. Although Jesus certainly loved the guy before he showed up, Mark is emphasizing that Jesus' intentional consideration of the young man tapped into the love Jesus had for him.

Just last night, my wife and I (Lance) sat in our second-story library, enjoying a glass of wine and music. She was looking across the street toward the home of our neighbor Jess. Last weekend his wife, Linda, had passed away after suf-fering for the last few years from Alzheimer's disease. Tears welled up in Sherri's eyes. "I've been staring at the lights in Jess's living room. He's in there—alone. I can't imagine how it must be for him." Sherri was *beholding* Jess. She was also planning how we could reach out to him.

Most often beholding comes before compassion. It is not

that we are not compassionate people, but we often are not *moved* with compassion because we don't "behold" others. Consider the following passages (from the KJV, with emphasis added) that include the phrase "moved with compassion":

> But when he saw the multitudes, he was *moved with compassion* on them, because they fainted, and were scattered abroad, as sheep having no shepherd.
>
> MATTHEW 9:36

> And Jesus went forth, and saw a great multitude, and was *moved with compassion* toward them, and he healed their sick.
>
> MATTHEW 14:14

The pace of our lives and consumer agendas greatly cloud our ability to *behold* others. Recently my wife and I were walking through downtown San Louis Obispo. As we approached a street corner, on our right we both saw a young man—probably in his midtwenties—who obviously was living on the street. He scurried to a trashcan and grabbed a Starbucks cup that was sitting on top of it and quickly drank what was left in the cup. He then began rummaging through the rubbish in search of scrap food to eat.

In my hand was a container of leftover dessert from a fine meal we had just enjoyed. I quickly handed it to him and pulled out the meager three dollars in cash I had with me. What caught both Sherri and me off-guard, though, were his eyes. They were filled with desperation and despair. We come across people begging on the streets just about everywhere we go, and we frequently give to such folks. This young man was not even begging. We beheld the young man and have been held by his eyes ever since. I am reminded here of the words of Frederick Buechner:

> If we are to love our neighbors, before doing anything else we must *see* our neighbors. With our imagination as well as our eyes, that is to say like artists, we must see not just their faces but the life behind and within their faces. Here it is love that is the frame we see them in.[6]

I'm enough of a knucklehead that often I need the plainest of translations or paraphrases to get what the Scriptures are trying to say. I love Eugene Peterson's take on Romans 13:8—"Don't run up debts, except for the huge debt of love you owe each other. When you love others, you complete what the law has been after all along." There is no such thing as debt-free living for a Christian. I owe you love right now. I can show you love this very second, but a minute from now, I will still owe you love.

Author Mike Mason writes,

> Every person we meet is God's representative to us, looking to collect His dues. Are we paying up? Are we paying "the continuing debt to love" (Romans

13:8)? Or do we treat God's people with the civilized equivalent of killing and beating: ignoring them, isolating ourselves, sitting in silent judgment, rationalizing our lovelessness?[7]

Getting to know our neighbors, the employees and frequent fellow customers at our favorite coffee shop, gym, or pizza parlor comes part and parcel with the call of God on our lives to love our neighbor as ourselves. Loving starts with knowing, and knowing starts with *getting to know*.

When my wife and I moved into our current neighborhood, the man who lived in the house behind ours was described by other neighbors as crazy and unfriendly. His house was unkempt and in extreme disrepair. And "Crazy Dan" was just as broken-down-looking as his home. We approached Dan, and after having him for meals in our home, my wife and I agreed he wasn't crazy. He certainly wasn't unfriendly. In fact, he was a really fun and wise person. A retired university professor, he was just lonely and a bit eccentric. But the labels others had put upon him served to push him into the recesses of the community. The "crazy" label became a category that cut him off from the life of the neighborhood. The definitions not only denied Dan the interaction he needed but also the gift he could be to the community.

A few months after Dan had to move to an assisted living complex, I ran into a couple who had been caring for his yard for several years. They told me a story that most of our neighbors would have been astounded to learn. When this couple first met Dan, they were homeless. They began doing odd jobs for him, and for almost two years Dan paid the rent on a home for them until they were back on their feet. Not only was Dan not crazy, but he also had a huge heart for others. Who would have known? Just the ones who took the time and effort to get to know.

Reflection and Preparation

- Do the neighbor's name challenge from earlier in the chapter. How many neighbors around your home do you know by name?
- When was the last time you had a conversation of five minutes or more with one of your neighbors?
- Consider taking some time over the next week to *behold* your neighbors. Sit down and think deeply about their lives in light of what you know about them.
- At the end of each day this week, think back on the people you encountered face to face. What comes to mind as you *behold* them?

- 6 -

Never Met a Stranger

THE POWER OF BIBLICAL HOSPITALITY

Do not forget to show hospitality to strangers, for by so doing some people have shown hospitality to angels without knowing it.

HEBREWS 13:2

If there is any concept worth restoring to its original depth and evocative potential, it is the concept of hospitality.

HENRI NOUWEN

The opposite of cruelty is not simply freedom from the cruel relationship, it is hospitality.

PHILIP HALLIE

WHAT IS THE FIRST THING that comes to mind when you hear the word *hospitality*? For most people, images emerge of entertaining around meals or inviting friends into our homes for a night of fun and games. Now let's be clear. There is nothing wrong with sharing a meal with friends and family. In fact, in the next chapter we will examine the significance of meals around a common table. Genuine, biblical hospitality, however, is much more than entertaining.

One simple distinction between biblical hospitality and entertaining is that the latter puts the focus on the host. In doing so it can actually become an issue of pride. As the host, we are concerned about what others will think about our home. We wonder how our home literally reflects on us. There is a desire to impress our guests. We want them to like us and the place we live. We worry about making everything just right. If our home isn't perfectly clean and decorated, how can we possibly entertain guests? This sort of hospitality can easily become more about *appearances* than *persons*.

With genuine, biblical hospitality, the focus is not on us as hosts. Instead, it is on the guest. Our concern is not on the appearance of our homes but on the needs and concerns of those invited into our homes. What do we have to learn from our guests? What do they have to share? What needs do our guests bring with them that we can address? What promise are they carrying with them that we need to receive? What about our guests can we celebrate during our time together? Soon, we discover, the distinction between host and guest proves to be artificial. Our differences evaporate into a mutual sense of being included.

Scripture gives further clarity on the concept of hospitality, as well as its crucial importance. The Bible holds hospitality—especially toward strangers—in high regard. The laws prescribing holiness in the book of Leviticus include references to hospitality:

> When a foreigner resides among you in your land,
> do not mistreat them. The foreigner residing among
> you must be treated as your native-born. Love them   ·

as yourself, for you were foreigners in Egypt. I am
the LORD your God.

LEVITICUS 19:33-34

We are not only to do no wrong to those outside of
our community; we are to actively love the "foreigner" as
we love ourselves. In this passage, the better translation of
"as yourself" (*kamocha*) is "for he is like you." We too were
aliens once—outside the community—yet God treated us as
native-born. The point is reiterated in Deuteronomy 10:19:
"You are to love those who are foreigners, for you yourselves
were foreigners in Egypt."

In the New Testament, this mandate is given with even more
force, as Jesus teaches in the parable of the sheep and the goats:

> Then the King will say to those on his right, "Come,
> you who are blessed by my Father; take your
> inheritance, the kingdom prepared for you since the
> creation of the world. For I was hungry and you gave
> me something to eat, I was thirsty and you gave me
> something to drink, I was a stranger and you invited
> me in, I needed clothes and you clothed me, I was
> sick and you looked after me, I was in prison and
> you came to visit me."
>
> Then the righteous will answer him, "Lord, when
> did we see you hungry and feed you, or thirsty and
> give you something to drink? When did we see you
> a stranger and invite you in, or needing clothes and

clothe you? When did we see you sick or in prison
and go to visit you?"

The King will reply, "Truly I tell you, whatever
you did for one of the least of these brothers and
sisters of mine, you did for me."

MATTHEW 25:34-40

To welcome the stranger is to welcome Christ. "Believer
or nonbeliever, attractive or unattractive, admirable or dis-
reputable, upstanding or vile—the stranger is marked by the
image of God."[1] Therefore, we are called to love. The Greek
word for hospitality in the New Testament makes this perfectly clear. It is the word *philoxenia*, which is a combination
of two words: love (*phileo*) and the word for stranger (*xenos*).
It literally means "love of stranger."

Loving the stranger was a vital element in the life of the
early church. There are numerous passages that speak to the
importance of hospitality. Just a few include:

Rejoice in hope, be patient in suffering, persevere in
prayer. Contribute to the needs of the saints; extend
hospitality to strangers.

ROMANS 12:12-13, NRSV

Do not forget to show hospitality to strangers, for
by so doing some people have shown hospitality to
angels without knowing it.

HEBREWS 13:2

The overseer is to be above reproach, faithful to
his wife, temperate, self-controlled, respectable,
hospitable, able to teach.

1 TIMOTHY 3:2

Offer hospitality to one another without grumbling.

1 PETER 4:9

There is another aspect of hospitality that is important to
note. It is not just for the benefit of the other. There is also
something extraordinary that is gained when we receive the
stranger.

When you give a dinner or a banquet, do not invite
your friends or your brothers or your relatives or rich
neighbors, lest they also invite you in return and you
be repaid. But when you give a feast, invite the poor,
the crippled, the lame, the blind, and you will be
blessed, because they cannot repay you.

LUKE 14:12-14, ESV

The practice of biblical hospitality is unique because it
reaches out to those who cannot reciprocate. In most cases
when we invite friends into our homes for dinner, there is an
expectation that they will return the "favor" and have us into
their home. But the point of this passage is that customary
"pay back" hospitality is of no great merit to God. The very
best hospitality is that which is bestowed, not exchanged.

The Jewish philosopher Emmanuel Levinas said that the only thing that really converts people at a deep level is seeing "the face of the other." Welcoming and empathizing with the other leads to transformation of the whole person. This interchange is prepared to transform both persons—the seer and the seen.[2] In a sense, we need the stranger for our own conversion from our individualism, self-centeredness, and tendencies towards self-preservation and exclusion.

Being included is really at the core of biblical hospitality. If we had to take all of this talk about loving strangers and welcoming people into our lives and homes, and boil it all down into one word, it would be the word *inclusion*. As followers of Jesus, we are called to be radically inclusive people. We should be quick to include others into our lives.

The opposite of inclusion is exclusion, which always involves dismissal and rejection. Can you remember a time in your life when you were excluded? Stop and think for a moment. How did being excluded from the lives and activities of others make you feel? Being left out, rejected by others, is deeply hurtful. The sad reality is that thousands of people live daily lives of exclusion. They are not welcomed—by anyone. They are left to exist at the margins, on the fringes of society, living relationally impoverished lives. It is not right. No one is brought into this world to live a life of isolation:

> "We do not flourish as human beings when we know
> no one and no one knows us; we do not flourish
> as human beings when we belong to no place and

no place cares about us. When we have no sense of relationship to people or place, we have no sense of responsibility to people or place."[3]

We are created as social, relational beings who are made for community. Hospitality, when rightly understood and pursued, has the power to break the bonds of isolation and exclusion.

Exclusion is not the way of Jesus. But if hospitality is clearly presented in Scripture, and if it gives us the capacity to overcome the relational separation that is so prevalent today, then why do we continue to exclude others? When did we lose the capacity to give and receive hospitality? Why has it virtually disappeared from the life of the church? The reasons are undoubtedly complex, but let's consider two of the greatest enemies of hospitality: fear and lack of margin.

Xenophobia

In sharp contrast to the Greek word *philoxenia*, which means "love of stranger," you may have heard the more popular word *xenophobia*, which is the fear or even hatred of the stranger or foreigner. While there is certainly a clinical expression of *xenophobia*, there is a level of fear of the stranger that has unfortunately been conditioned in us all throughout time.

The authors of *Radical Hospitality: Benedict's Way of Love* speak to the damaging effect fear has on our ability to welcome the stranger:

Fear is a thief. It will steal our peace of mind. . . . But it also hijacks relationships, keeping us sealed up in our plastic world with a fragile sense of security.

Being a people who fear the stranger, we have drained the life juices out of hospitality. The hospitality we explore here . . . is not about sipping tea and making bland talk with people who live next door or work with you. Hospitality is a lively, courageous, and convivial way of living that challenges our compulsion either to turn away or to turn inward and disconnect ourselves from others.[4]

Author and futurist Faith Popcorn has labeled the current phenomenon of decreased socializing as "cocooning." In an increasingly alienating social climate, "we've become preoccupied with creating warm and safe home environments in which the realities and challenges of the outside world are kept away."[5]

The average American, middle-class family has increasingly become a place to achieve safety and security from the "dangers" of secular society. The home has become a stronghold to protect the family from the evils of the world, rather than a place of welcome and hospitality. Writing on the typical American view of the home, Deb Hirsch provides this powerful critique:

This is "our" space, and those we may "invite" into that space are carefully chosen based on whether they will upset the delicate status quo, inconvenience us, or pose a threat to our perceived safety. In other words, visitors, especially strange ones, stress us out. And while this is in some sense culturally understandable, the negative result in terms of our spirituality is that the family has effectively become a pernicious idol. . . . Culture has once again trumped our social responsibility. In such a situation, missional hospitality is seen as a threat, not as an opportunity to extend the kingdom; so an idol (a sphere of life dissociated from the claims of God) is born. . . .

Our families and our homes should be places where people can experience a foretaste of heaven, where the church is rightly viewed as a community of the redeemed from all walks of life (Revelation 21). Instead, our fears restrict us from letting go of the control and safety we have spent years cultivating.[6]

We wrongly assume that one of the greatest needs in our lives is safety. But what we need most is connection and acceptance from other human beings. Locks and fences can never do for our withered souls what genuine friendships can. Fear is indeed a thief. It will steal our ability to forge new relationships. Instead we must see hospitality as an adventure that takes us to places we never dreamed of going.

My (Brad's) family knows this firsthand. There was a day our family bought into the notion that our home was our castle. It was our personal space that ought not be intruded upon. While we had people in our home on a regular basis, it was almost always at our convenience. In other words, we opened our home when the time and circumstances were a good fit for us.

This was true up until a few years ago, when we began to rethink the use of our home. Our family decided to convert a home office back to a bedroom to be in a better position to welcome others into our home. We then took the necessary steps to become a foster family. Over the past several years, we have provided emergency care to more than seventy children at risk, some for only a few days, others for several weeks.

When talking about our foster care story I will often share three benefits of providing care. First, it is a wonderful way to influence the lives of children. Second, in many cases there is a great opportunity to influence the lives of the parent or parents, who in most circumstances is a single mother. But third, providing care to these children is the single best thing we have ever done for our own kids. We have learned how God uses hospitality to shape and form us. That is a fascinating aspect of kingdom living. As you bestow a blessing for the benefit of others, you realize that you too are a recipient of God's grace.

Hospitality is about making room in our lives for others. It encompasses friends, neighbors, and especially strangers. It is really about seeing strangers become friends. With practice, hospitality can become a way of life, one that helps us to follow more closely the ways of Jesus, but also one that will continue to transform our view of the other.

When we fear the other, our own world gets smaller and smaller. It is only when we open our homes and our lives to the stranger that we can see our world begin to enlarge. The real question is not "How dangerous is that stranger?" The real question is, how dangerous will I become if I am not more open?

No Margin

While fear is certainly a significant hindrance to becoming more hospitable, the second and perhaps greater barrier has to do with time—or what we refer to as lack of margin.

How ridiculous would it be if the pages of a book had no margin? In the book *Margin: Restoring Emotional, Physical, Financial, and Time Reserves to Overloaded Lives*, author Richard Swenson provides this excellent metaphor for overburdened lives. What would be your opinion of a publisher that "tried to cram the print top to bottom and side to side so that every blank space was filled up? The result would be aesthetically displeasing and chaotic"—much like many of our lives.[7]

Margin is the space between our load and our limits, between vitality and fatigue. It is the opposite of overload, and therefore the remedy for that troublesome condition.[8]

[Margin] is this space that guarantees sustainability. It is in this space where healing occurs, where our batteries are recharged, where our relationships are nourished, and where wisdom is found. Without margin, both rest and contemplation are but theoretical concepts, unaffordable and unrealistic. We do not follow two inches behind the next car on the interstate—that would leave no margin for error. We do not allow only two minutes to change planes in Chicago—that would be foolish in the extreme. We do not load boats until they are nearly submerged— that would invite disaster. Why then do we insist on leaving no buffer, no space, no reserves in our day-to-day?[9]

This metaphor is helpful when considering the ideas of neighboring and hospitality because *relationships happen in the margins*. When there is no margin it is impossible to welcome others into our lives. Hospitality cannot be added to already overburdened lives.

Without margin, we are incapable of relational spontaneity in our neighborhood. Without margin, we are uninterested in opportunities to serve our neighbors. Without margin, we are unable to even think about planning time to spend with others. Margin creates buffers. It gives us room to breathe, freedom to act, and time to adapt. "Only then will we be able to nourish our relationships. Only then will we be available and interruptible for the purposes of God."[10]

What can we do to create margin? How can I rethink my day so there is time for relationships to flourish?

Alignment

When people are first challenged with the exhortation to love their neighbor and to find ways to be more hospitable, there is often a cloud of anxiety. How in the world is a person supposed to add more activities to an already busy week? Part of the answer is to think about *alignment* rather than *addition*. In other words, instead of stressing out about adding more relational activities to a packed schedule, we need to consider how to align the rhythms of our lives alongside the rhythms of others.

For example, most people eat twenty-one meals a weeks. What would it look like to align two or three of those meals in such a way that you eat with others? Maybe it is breakfast or lunch out? Or perhaps once a week you ask someone in the neighborhood over for dinner.

> Jesus' hospitality to the displaced and distressed was not calculated but casual. It is as though Jesus lived his life as a type of present participle: as he was going. . . . By adopting the vision of Jesus, by seeing as and how Jesus sees, our inclination toward hospitality will become natural and unforced. Hospitality ought to be ad hoc and personal.[11]

In many cases we have found it especially easy to invite people for dessert after dinner. Either way, we look for activities we are doing already and simply ask others to join us.

Audit

A second step that many of us need to take is to do a *margin audit* of our time. Margin is not something that just happens. You have to plan for it. In a culture that applauds ambition and perpetual activity, you will actually have to fight for it. It is rare to see a life prescheduled to less than 100 percent. But if we want to live hospitable lives that have space to invite others into, we must learn to plan our lives at less than full capacity.

We need to take a serious look at our schedule to examine what an average week looks like. In the book *Time Traps*, author Tom Duncan argues for the need of a time budget. The idea is similar to a financial budget; the only difference is that you plan how you will spend your time rather than money. Map it out. Just as you would with your finances, identify where you spend your time. Are you overloaded? Does your schedule provoke anxiety? Is there margin where new relationships could be cultivated?

Perhaps you simply need permission to stop. Maybe you need to hear that is okay to say no.

> Saying No is not just a good idea—it has now become a mathematical necessity. Without this two-letter word, I doubt that regaining margin is possible. If there are fifteen good things to do today and you can do only ten of them, you will need to say No five times.[12]

"No," says author Anne Lamott, "is a complete sentence."[13] You simply don't have to say yes to everything.

Paradoxically, in our pursuit of margin we must learn to slow down—to be unhurried. John Ortberg says we "must ruthlessly eliminate hurry from our lives."[14] When Jesus says, "Follow me," he isn't inviting us into a race. Instead he is welcoming us into a life-giving relationship with him that should affect all of our relationships. As followers of Jesus, we should be in the best position—spiritually and time wise—to love our neighbors. But often we let the ways of the world dictate our time rather than the ways of Jesus.

Next time you read the story of the Good Samaritan (Luke 10:30-37), consider it from the perspective of margin.

> The priest and Levite may well have been returning from temple service and were concerned about becoming ceremonially unclean. They were about to be engaged in doing God's work and were, perhaps, in a hurry to remain faithful to it. They saw the wounded man as a distraction from what they were supposed to do for God.[15]

Maybe their schedules were so full they simply couldn't accommodate a wounded person on the way. There just wasn't time to spare before their next religious duty. Lack of margin not only can keep us from stopping, it can keep us from even noticing what is really going on in the lives of those around us. What are some practical steps to cultivate margin so we don't pass by what God may be calling us to do? Here are a few simple actions we have taken to help create margin in our own family.

First, we match calendars often. At least once a week, my wife and I (Brad) compare our calendars. Do we know when and where each other will be throughout the week? We see where we might need to carve out time. What days will be unusually busy? What days or partial days do I need to make sure I don't schedule anything?

Second, we never have any of our kids playing different sports at the same time. There was a season of life were I was going one direction with one kid and my wife was going the opposite direction with another kid. We decided right then that each child needed to pick one sport for the year or that the sports had to be in the same geographical location. We refer to it as pruning the activity branches. If we are serious about creating margin, there will be times that something will need to be cut off.

Third, I work really hard to schedule no evening meetings. In fact, I will not even schedule a meeting late in the day if there is a chance it will run into the early evening. I start everything early to make sure our evenings are open to hang out in our neighborhood.

Fourth, we take lots of walks in the neighborhood. When we do, we try to recapture the ancient art of *strolling*. We make sure we are not in a hurry. We stop often. Observe. Talk, listen and engage with those in our neighborhood who we encounter along the way.

Finally, to practice slowing we set aside no- or at least low-tech times in our schedules. Alan Fadling writes, "I almost always have a phone in my pocket, an iPad in my briefcase and a computer on my desk. This ever-present technology has a way of accelerating my inner life. My mobile phone makes me virtually omnipresent: I'm nearly *always* available."[16]

There is a simple practice that I (Brad) have incorporated into my daily rhythm of work that has helped me to at least partially tame the tech monster. While I work out of several coffee shops around the city, I have one particular hangout that I frequent three to four times a week. To enact a sense of slowing, a sense of resting in that place, I force myself to sit without my computer or phone for the first fifteen minutes of every visit. No matter how much work I have to do, or how urgent a looming task may seem, I refuse to take my phone out of my pocket or my laptop out of my bag. I simply establish a posture of slowing. I sit quietly. I observe. I listen. I ask what God is doing in this place, at this time. Is there something he wants me to do before I reach for my computer? In a sense, it is a self-imposed block of margin. Where in your daily routine can you force yourself to slow down and create space for those around you?

God will honor our efforts to make hospitality a regular rhythm of life, and Jesus will reward all who serve him through welcoming the hungry, the thirsty, the stranger, the sick, and the imprisoned. "We can celebrate the fact that every time people sit down to eat and drink together, there is the possibility that community will grow, people will be reconciled to one another, and we will gain new perceptions of God's inclusive love. That is good news for a broken, fractured, and polarized world."[17] The only thing getting in the way of living radically hospitable lives is our willingness to open our hearts, arms, and homes.

Reflection and Preparation

Immerse. Reflect on the following quote from Mother Teresa: "We think sometimes that poverty is only being hungry, naked and homeless. The poverty of being unwanted, unloved and uncared for is the greatest poverty."

Recognize your resources. Where do you have space in your home and in your life that could be opened up to the other? Do you have room in your heart to love and serve someone who is unwanted, unloved, and uncared for? Do you have room in your home to welcome someone, even temporarily?

Consider others. Who in your neighborhood, your place of work, or the places in which you hang out is living a relationally impoverished life? How can you turn a stranger into a friend this week?

Pray. Begin to pray that God would give you fresh eyes to see those who are unwanted, unloved, and uncared for, that he would give you the courage to do whatever it takes to live out the essence of biblical hospitality and love the stranger.

Meals on Heels

THE BIG DEAL ABOUT EATING TOGETHER

He brought me to the banqueting house,
and his banner over me was love.

SONG OF SOLOMON 2:4, ESV

Preparing and cooking, serving and eating meals are
Jesus-sanctioned activities that provide daily structure to our
participation in the work of salvation.

EUGENE PETERSON,
CHRIST PLAYS IN TEN THOUSAND PLACES

The Son of Man came eating and drinking.

JESUS

AMONG THE MANY HEAD-SHAKING QUOTES attributed to the legendary baseballer Yogi Berra, he is supposed to have said, "You can observe a lot just by watching." True. It is not enough to just listen to Jesus. We need to watch him as well. We can discover quite a bit about the way to reach others by looking at how Jesus did it. Describing his own *modus operandi* for reaching a broken world, he didn't say, "The Son of Man came with Bible in hand." He didn't say, "I came with a sword" or "I came with a list of dos and don'ts." No. Jesus said, "I came with a fork and wine glass."

Two of the most notable miracles Jesus performed were

centered around food and drink. His first miracle kept a party going. When the father of the bride found himself in an embarrassing situation at a wedding, one that no Jewish father wanted to be found in, Jesus bailed him out—and he bailed him out lavishly. In those days it was commonly expected that the father of the bride had been storing up wine for the entirety of his little girl's life, in preparation for the wedding day, where it would lubricate the guests. To run out of wine was unthinkable. Jesus called for six ceremonial water jugs to be filled with water, and he turned it all into wine. The math on this miracle equates to just less than one thousand bottles of wine! And this was not some Boone's Farm swill either. It was the best wine anyone had ever tasted.

The first miracle of Jesus most of us learned about in childhood is the feeding of the five thousand, where he takes a few loaves of bread and a couple of fish and feeds thousands of people. So, yeah, Jesus came eating and drinking! And to top it all off, he says, "Here is how I want you to remember me: eat and drink" (see Luke 22:19-20).

The Gospel accounts corroborate what Jesus had to say about his method of operation. Eating and drinking with others is a constant theme throughout the biblical history of how and what Jesus did during his earthly ministry. Churches are most often found meeting. Jesus was most often found eating. If you were to bump into him on the streets of Jerusalem, he would have been more likely to invite you to a barbecue than to a Bible study. If we were to edit out all the content of the Gospels that involved Jesus eating with others, we would have very little left of what Jesus said and did. It's probably a good thing he did all that walking around Jerusalem, or he may have become a bit chunky.

Robert Karris, in his book *Eating Your Way through Luke's Gospel*, observes that "in Luke . . . Jesus is either going to a meal, at a meal, or coming from a meal."[1] In his excellent little book (which we heartedly recommend) *A Meal with Jesus*, Tim Chester points out the many occasions of Jesus eating with others just within Luke's Gospel:

- Chapter 5—Jesus eats with tax collectors and sinners at the home of Levi.
- Chapter 7—Jesus is anointed at the home of Simon the Pharisee during a meal.
- Chapter 9—Jesus feeds the five thousand.
- Chapter 10—Jesus eats in the home of Martha and Mary.
- Chapter 11—Jesus condemns the Pharisees and teachers of the law at a meal.
- Chapter 14—Jesus is at a meal when he urges people to invite the poor rather than their friends to their meals.
- Chapter 19—Jesus invites himself to dinner with Zacchaeus.
- Chapter 22—Jesus hosts the Last Supper.
- Chapter 24—The risen Christ has a meal with the two disciples in Emmaus and then later eats fish with the disciples in Jerusalem.

Contrast this pattern in Jesus' life with contemporary society. It has already been a decade and a half since Robert Putnam identified a 45 percent decline in entertaining friends at home since the 1960s. The downward trend continues. A recent *New York Times* article titled "Guess Who Isn't Coming to Dinner" focused on the lost art, and even the lost desire, for throwing dinner parties. Busy schedules, the inconvenience of planning, and even the lack of knowing how to cook are reasons given as to the loss of conviviality among Americans.[2] In an article titled "Are Dinner Parties a Thing of the Past?" we read,

> Many of the folks interviewed hinted towards the fact that they're from a different time, a time when schedules were a little looser and people were more interested in the pomp and circumstance of the dinner party. More young couples received nice china on their wedding day, and tableware and silverware were carefully collected.[3]

In many cases, eating *in* has been supplanted by eating *out*. For the first time ever, sales at restaurants and bars overtook spending at grocery stores in 2015.[4] Though the millennial generation receives a lot of credit for this change, they actually love being in the kitchen—76 percent of millennials say they like to cook.[5] But many of them have to learn their way around a kitchen because no one ever taught them how to cook.

Evangelistically Eating

Eugene Peterson poses an important question:

> Is it significant that Luke, who has more references
> in his Gospel to "save" and "salvation" . . . also has
> the most references to Jesus at meals or telling stories
> of meals? I think so. Luke's Gospel, in comparison
> to those of his Gospel-writing colleagues, is tilted in
> the direction of evangelism, making the connection
> between the message of salvation in history and the
> outsiders of history.[6]

If there is any such thing as an evangelistic tool, we are convinced that the most powerful evangelistic tool—the one Jesus used more than any—is something 99.9 percent of Christians have in their homes: a dining table. And yet Christians, though they sincerely want to reach others with the Good News of the kingdom, seldom invite others to share meals. It is as if we figure that something so earthy could never play into something so heavenly. We have exchanged the most natural, relational, and disarming process imaginable for awkward, pretentious, and sophomoric evangelistic gimmicks and presentations. Eugene Peterson continues:

> The practice of hospitality has fallen on bad times.
> Fewer and fewer families sit down to a meal together.
> The meal, which used to be a gathering place for

families, neighbors, and "the stranger at the gate," is
on its way out. Given the prominence of the Supper
in our worshiping lives, the prominence of meals in
the Jesus work of salvation, it is surprising how little
notice is given among us to the relationship between
the Meal and our meals. Our surprise develops into
a sense of urgency when we recognize that a primary,
maybe *the* primary, venue for evangelism in Jesus' life
was the meal. Is Jesus' preferred setting for playing
out the work of salvation on this field of history only
marginally available to us? By marginalizing meals of
hospitality in our daily lives have we inadvertently
diminished the work of evangelism? And is there
anything to be done about it?[7]

Leonard Sweet says the best definition of the gospel comes
from Jean Leclerc: "Jesus ate good food with bad people."[8]
Jesus consistently gave the "in" crowd lessons on relationship as he was hanging out at mixers and potluck dinners,
mingling with the "out" crowd. When he saw the tax collector, Zacchaeus (whom I can't help but believe was Danny
DeVito's doppelganger) up in a tree and trying to get a
glimpse of him, Jesus invited himself to dinner at his house.
On another occasion we find Jesus with yet another tax collector and his sketchy buddies, hanging out around a meal.

When the Pharisees saw him keeping this kind of
company, they had a fit, and lit into Jesus' followers.

"What kind of example is this from your Teacher,
acting cozy with crooks and riffraff?"
MATTHEW 9:10-11, MSG

Christians should be the partyingest people on the street.
The reason we are not could be that we just flat out do not
know *how* to throw a party. Seriously. Our buddy Hugh
Halter includes "party throwing" in some of the training talks
he does about how to reach others. He says that people often
ask, "How do you start?" Hugh sarcastically widens his eyes
and slowly says, "First. Answer the door. Then. Open the
door. Then . . ."

Jesus didn't reveal a new character trait of God with all his
feasting. The partying side of God was well known among
the Jewish people. Throughout the history of Israel a multitude of feasts were scattered throughout the year in which the
people of God were commanded to participate. In Leviticus
23 we see the Lord command seven feasts (parties) across the
calendar year. Additionally, God commanded another tithe
to cover the expenses of these feasts.

You shall tithe all the yield of your seed that comes
from the field year by year. And before the LORD
your God, in the place that he will choose, to make
his name dwell there, you shall eat the tithe of
your grain, of your wine, and of your oil, and the
firstborn of your herd and flock, that you may learn
to fear the LORD your God always. And if the way

is too long for you, so that you are not able to carry the tithe, when the LORD your God blesses you, because the place is too far from you, which the LORD your God chooses, to set his name there, then you shall turn it into money and bind up the money in your hand and go to the place that the LORD your God chooses and spend the money for whatever you desire—oxen or sheep or wine or strong drink, whatever your appetite craves. And you shall eat there before the LORD your God and rejoice, you and your household.

DEUTERONOMY 14:22-26, ESV

Do you remember the last time you heard a sermon on this tithe? Most likely you never have. Let this all sink in. First, God says, "I want you to frequently take time out and have a party. Some of these parties will last a day, and some will last a week." Next, he says, "Set aside 10 percent of your income and blow it on these celebrations!" To top it all off, the Lord says he wants his people to "spend the money for whatever you desire." How amazing is that? You want Cheetos? Get some. You want Oreos? Go for it. You want filet mignon? Load up. You want to hire Penn and Teller to entertain? Book 'em. You can almost hear Kool and the Gang singing behind this verse: "Celebrate good times, come on!" The Lord wants us to regularly and sumptuously celebrate his goodness with our families, our friends, and great food.

Bread Company

In 2003, shortly after the war in Afghanistan had begun, I (Lance) found myself sitting at the gates of an Afghani settlement, deep in Taliban-dominated Helmand Province. My American friends and I had been invited to meet with the village elders for a meal. We had bumped along in Toyota pickups for four hours to reach the remote location, accompanied by Afghani militants outfitted with machine guns and rocket-propelled grenades. We approached the village and saw more militants stationed around the place. I was beginning to want my mommy, and I asked one of my more experienced buddies how safe we were. He said, "You couldn't be anywhere safer in Afghanistan. The elders and the people have invited us to break bread with them. They would defend us to the death if needed."

Over the next couple of hours, we enjoyed easy conversation while eating our fill from the bountiful harvest of our generous Afghani hosts. Within eyesight of the harvest fields and earshot of the bleating herd from which our meat was taken, elbows literally rubbed together and hands collided, dipping into the bowls of salads, relishes, fruits, handmade unleavened bread, and freshly roasted lamb. This ancient people, who possessed very little, had set before us their best. A better meal I cannot remember. A more welcoming meal I've never experienced.

The word *companion* is a conjunction of two Latin words: *cum,* which means "together," and *panis,* which means "bread." The conveyance is that we come together to eat with those who are our friends. When we take the precious produce we have labored over feeding and raising, planting, tending, cultivating, and preparing, and offer it to another, we are essentially giving a piece of our life to that person. Something sacred is present.

Even if we haven't raised the food we are offering to others, we have still worked by the sweat of our brow to be able to obtain it. Either way, a sacrifice is involved. The word *sacrifice* comes from the same root word as *sacred:* Sacrifice is essential to anything that is sacred. It is unfortunate that we have become so accustomed to calling Jimmy John's or Domino's Pizza, swiping our credit cards, and punching in our pin numbers that we have lost the sacred significance behind breaking bread with others.

It's Just Too Easy

For several years some friends of ours from Lexington, Kentucky, have been regular participants in a fantastic weekly bread gathering—or, more precisely, a *cornbread* gathering. They call it Cornbread Suppers.

The Cornbreadians, as they call themselves, have been gathering for several years at the behest of a couple who simply wanted to get to know their neighbors and decided to do something about it. They wanted something that folks could depend upon on a weekly basis. According to founders Rona Roberts and Steve Kay, the "rules" are simple:

- You can bring anything or anyone you like.
- You don't have to bring anything or anyone.
- You can bring a bottle or a dish.
- No program and no agenda. Just eat, talk, laugh, and trade stories.
- No RSVPs necessary.
- All are welcome.

Our friends had told us about Cornbread Suppers a couple of years back, and my wife and I (Lance) decided to try it in our neighborhood. We are signed up on a social media site for our local neighborhood, and I sent out a brief inquiry to see if any of our neighbors would be interested. Within minutes the responses started rolling in. They continued for the next several days:

- "Oh this is wonderful. Yes, please include us."
- "I love it! Let me know when this starts."
- "We would absolutely be interested! What a terrific idea! Please keep us posted with details."
- "Yes! I would be very interested. We all should know each other better!"
- "An excellent concept! My wife and I would love to be a part of it!"
- "What a fantastic idea! It builds many good things, not the least of which is a sense of community and neighborliness. So very cool."

Notice all those exclamation points in the responses. Neighboring is a lost art, but people have not lost a heart for it. Not by a long shot. Within a couple of weeks we hosted our own inaugural Cornbread Supper. That was a year ago, and if we stopped it now, there would be a major revolt. Most of those who participate host the Cornbread Supper from time to time, and we have done all kinds of differing themes: Italian-food night, Mexican-food night, Asian-food night, and a progressive-dessert night. We have developed new friendships all across our neighborhood that we had not had in the previous five years of living here. And our neighbors have developed friendships as well. I can say this has been the easiest and most neighborhood-transformative thing Sherri and I have ever been a part of. We have shared our story with several others who have started their own neighborhood Cornbread Suppers, and they have had similar experiences with it.

Beauty and the Feast

In the late-1980s film *Babette's Feast*, an unlikely heroine emerges in the form of a refugee who has lost her son and husband in the French civil war. The setting for the tale is a dreary coastal village in Denmark. An old dean who rules over a local Lutheran church sets an austere tone, renouncing and forbidding all hint of earthly pleasure. His two daughters, once ravishing beauties, have become elderly matrons who struggle to continue the mission of their late father, but in the time since his passing the church has fragmented severely. Gossip and rumor, whispers and accusations, stoke the embers of feuds, suspicions, and disagreements on mostly trite and molehill-like matters. Brothers feud. A couple of old women play a game of the silent treatment. And two church members suffer the guilt of a decades-long buzz of a sexual affair.

All the while, the church continues to hold services each Sabbath. In honor of their vows to live a pleasureless life, the sect members all wear black. Their diet consists of boiled cod and a gruel made from boiling bread in water fortified with a splash of ale.[9]

Babette arrives at the village on a blustery and rainy night, collapsing from exhaustion at the door of the two sisters. Not speaking Danish, she hands them a letter which they quickly discover is from a former forbidden love of one of the sisters from days long past. He is now a famous opera singer in France. The Frenchman requests that the sisters provide Babette quarters. "Babette can cook," he writes. Over the next dozen years, Babette serves the sisters, basically, as a maid and cook. Dutifully she cooks the cod and gruel, per her assignment.

Unknown to any of the villagers is her past experience as a cook in the renowned Café Anglis. One day Babette receives a letter—the first in her entire twelve-year stay in the village. She has won ten thousand francs in the French lottery. The sisters rejoice with Babette for her incredible fortune but are forlorn on the inside: They are certain that this will mean she will soon be leaving. Babette has other ideas.

The sisters have recently been discussing plans to celebrate their late father's hundredth birthday. Babette comes to them with a request: She wants to prepare an authentic French dinner for the celebration. Visions of snails, horsemeat, and other disgusting French fare overtake the imaginations of the sisters. Nevertheless, Babette has never asked anything of them during her entire servitude, and now here she is, wanting to serve them at her own expense. How could they possibly say no?

After she receives her winnings, Babette sets upon making arrangements for her feast. Over the next several weeks the villagers are treated to sights they have never witnessed, as provisions of all sorts begin to arrive at the port, then move through the streets to Babette's kitchen. Truffles, sea creatures, birds, vegetables, and all other manner of animal parts arrive, along with exotic fruits. Prospective guests for the approaching feast are horrified. Yes, the French are indeed mad. Just look at what they eat.

On a mid-December day, the village betrays its usual dreary persona, enraptured in the cloak of freshly fallen, glistening snow. Babette has cobbled together enough tableware and decor to set a gorgeous table. Though they were at odds among themselves, the Lutherans have agreed to choke down the meal without murmuring, lest they offend Babette.

As if by magic, a thaw begins to overtake the diners. Confessions begin to be exchanged, feuds are instantly dissolved, and joy brings color to the scene. Babette's feast has brought restoration and reconciliation. The price is all of her winnings: She will remain a member of this (new) community.

Jesus came eating and drinking. Let us be followers of Jesus.

Reflection and Preparation

So, start dreaming! What are the possibilities around your table or outdoor grill?

Progressive dinners. Come up with a theme (Italian, Asian, homestyle American), and have neighbors host a course of the meal at their place. Everyone moves from house to house, or apartment to apartment, and eats the course prepared by that host.

Cooking or recipe-swap nights. Each person brings a prepared dish plus copies of the recipe to share. Themes can be built around holidays, a particular required ingredient, or something that includes the telling of the story behind the dish ("My grandma fixed this every Sunday").

Wine tasting. Hold a wine-tasting evening. Everyone brings a favorite bottle of wine. Or invite a local sommelier to present some wines.

Cornbread Suppers. For more information, visit www .cornbreadsuppers.com/p/about-cornbread-suppers.html.

- 8 -

THE IMPORTANCE OF THIRD PLACES

Great civilizations, like great cities, share a common feature. Evolving within them and crucial to their growth and refinement are distinctive informal public gathering places.

RAY OLDENBURG, *THE GREAT GOOD PLACE*

Place gathers stories, relationships, memories.

EUGENE PETERSON

IN CHAPTER 1 we introduced a book by sociologist Ray Oldenburg titled *The Great Good Place*. We were paralleling the themes from the film *Avalon* with Oldenburg's contention that most American cities have lost the informal public life that once existed there. What we didn't mention in that earlier chapter was the one specific feature of community life that made up the primary focus of Oldenburg's research.

In his book Oldenburg coins the language of first, second, and third place. For Oldenburg, our first place is where we live, our second place is where we work, and our third place is a setting of common ground, or "hangout." The subtitle of the book provides further description of these third places: *Cafes, Coffee Shops, Community Centers, Beauty Parlors, General Stores, Bars, Hangouts, and How They Get You through the Day.*

In the most basic sense, a third place is a public setting that hosts regular, voluntary, and informal gatherings of people.[1] It is a place to relax, a place where people enjoy visiting. Third places provide the opportunity to know and be known. How are we to understand the distinctions of third places? How do you differentiate between these noteworthy hangouts and other gathering spots in a city? And what function do they play in the flourishing of a local community?

To begin, let's consider eight characteristics that Oldenburg identifies as being essential in the makeup of typical third places:

- *Neutral ground.* People are free to come and go as they please. No one person is required to play host. Everyone feels at home. There are no time requirements or invitations needed. Much of the time lived in first places (home) and second places (work) are structured, but not so in third places.
- *Acts as a leveler.* A third place is an inclusive place. It is accessible to the general public. People from all walks of life gather. There are no social or economic status barriers. While there is a tendency for individuals to select their associates and friends from among those closest to them in social rank, third places serve to expand possibilities, whereas formal associations tend

to narrow and restrict them. Worldly status claims must be checked at the door of third places in order for everyone to be equals.

- *Conversation is the main activity.* Nothing more clearly indicates a third place than that the talk is lively, stimulating, colorful, and engaging. Unlike corporate settings where status often dictates who may speak, and when and for how long, third places provide the environment for every voice to be heard.
- *Accessible and accommodating.* The best third places are those to which one may go at almost any time of the day or evening with assurance that acquaintances will be there. They tend to be conveniently located, often within walking distance of a person's home.
- *There are regulars.* What attracts regular visitors to a third place is not so much the establishment itself but the fellow customers. It is the regulars who give the third place its character and appeal. It is the regulars who set the tone of hospitality. And while it is easy to recognize who the regulars are, newcomers are welcomed into the group, unlike other places.
- *Low profile.* As a physical structure, third places are typically plain and unimpressive in appearance. They are not usually advertised. In most cases they are located in older buildings, partly because newer places tend to emerge in prime retail locations that come with expectations of high-volume customer traffic. This runs contrary to the essential need to linger. It is

in "hanging out" that people share conversation and life with one another.

- *Mood is playful.* With food, drink, games, and conversation present, the mood is light and good-natured. Joy and acceptance overrules anxiety and alienation. The mood encourages people to stay longer and to come back repeatedly.

- *A home away from home.* At their core, third places are where people feel at home. They feel like they belong there, and typically have a sense of ownership.

Oldenburg argues that between the often private worlds of home and work, we all need a third place to informally gather with our neighbors. Whether that place is a coffee shop, a pub, a café, or a beauty salon or barbershop, the important thing is that it is open to everyone.

In the late 1980s and early 1990s, one of the more popular shows on American television provided perhaps the most iconic example of Oldenburg's definition of a third place. The television series was called *Cheers,* after the name of a sports bar in the heart of Boston. One beloved scene took place in nearly every episode: When a particular "regular" would bust through the front door of the bar, everyone would shout his name in unison: "Norm!" The tagline for the show was "Where everybody knows your name."

If you are familiar with the show, you can easily reflect on each of Oldenburg's characteristics and see how the sports bar served as a quintessential third place. There was nothing fancy about the setting. Everyone was welcome. There were obviously regulars. Conversations were always spirited. And a beautiful picture of how the bar acted as a leveler, regardless of status or vocation, was demonstrated every week as the psychiatrist shared a beer and banter with the mailman.

But it is interesting to note that *Cheers* is not the only popular television program to integrate the life of the show's characters with that of a third place. We can find these places depicted in nearly every popular sitcom on television. Just consider a few examples over the past few decades.

- Floyd's Barbershop on *The Andy Griffith Show* is Mayberry's hangout for all the town's men.
- Arnold's is *the* hangout on the series *Happy Days*.
- Jerry, Kramer, Elaine, and George spend most of their informal time at Monk's Café on the series *Seinfeld*.
- Nipsey's Lounge is the group's favorite hangout on *Martin*.
- The popular coffee shop on the program *Friends* is Central Perk.
- Cooper's restaurant is a regular retreat on *King of Queens*.
- MacLaren's Pub is the go-to gathering spot on the comedy *How I Met Your Mother*.
- Even *Spongebob Squarepants* has the Krusty Krab.

The point of this very brief sampling is simply to illustrate how these public places are at the heart of a community's social vitality. If we desire to see our neighborhoods once again become abundant communities, then we must recognize the importance of third places, but also understand where and how to engage these public places. Let's begin by examining three different ways to view third places and then discuss how to respond to each.

Typical Third Places

Oldenburg's examples of third places include the local café, coffee shop, barbershop or beauty salon, and neighborhood pub. It's interesting that the word *pub* originates from the phrase "public house," which referred to a place that was open to the public, as opposed to a private dwelling. Like the local pub, these types of third places can be defined by each of the eight characteristics Oldenburg argues make up a genuine third place. That is why we call them *typical*.

One additional typical third place that is not mentioned in *The Great Good Place* is the present-day cigar shop. Regardless of what you think about smoking cigars, many people (especially men) have found these shops to be a great place to connect relationally. Our friend Dan Southerland, teaching pastor of Westside Family Church, one of the largest churches in Kansas City, is a huge cigar enthusiast. He not only enjoys a good cigar, but he also loves the opportunity it provides to build relationships with men who regularly hang out at one particular shop. Dan has been a regular at the cigar shop for so many years that everyone at the shop knows him as the "God guy." There are several men who are now connected to the church in some way because they first met Dan at the cigar shop.

Atypical Third Places

There are many places that would not fit Oldenburg's definition but still provide similar opportunities for significant interactions. It is important to broaden our understanding of third places to consider these *atypical* places.

Atypical third places are many. They can include the library, gym, laundromat, farmer's market, community garden, park, grocery store, shopping mall, and any other place that you and others frequent regularly. One of my (Brad's) favorite atypical third places is the local gym. I have gotten the opportunity to get to know nearly every person who works there and also dozens of other people who use the facility at the same time of the day.

One of my favorite atypical-third-place stories came from a woman who heard me speak about identifying public places at a training event in Southern California. She told me that she had noticed that parents at her children's elementary school would arrive thirty minutes early to simply hang out at the main entrance of the school as they waited for their children. After learning about third places, she realized that was exactly what was happening with this group of parents. They were coming together to make relational connections and get to know each other better. Right then she resolved to do the same. She intentionally began arriving early every day to get to know other parents. It didn't take long for her to begin to build a relationship with a single dad who happened to be Muslim. She discovered that he owned his own window-cleaning business. After a couple of weeks of cultivating the relationship, she asked whether he would be interested in taking on the job of washing the windows at her church. He was astonished that a Christian woman would make such an offer to a Muslim man. He accepted the job proposal, and over time the relationship was deepened. Eventually the man brought his children to the church's Easter service. I don't know how the story has unfolded since that Sunday, but all of it was made possible because this woman saw a place that others were gathering, and she decided to join them—to become one of the regulars.

Temporary Third Places

In addition to these typical and atypical third places, it is helpful to consider places that may have a limited life span. For example, think about a neighborhood swimming pool. Depending on the part of the country you live in, a pool may be open for only a few months out of the year. But during the summer the pool is transformed into a wonderful *temporary* third place. Each Saturday at our neighborhood pool, there are dozens of parents gathered around the water, keeping an eye on their children. It can provide a great opportunity to meet families in the neighborhood by simply asking where people live and which children "belong" to whom.

For my wife, the primary temporary third places are garage sales. It is amazing the number of times she will come home after a morning of checking out sales in the neighborhood to share with me the new relationships she has made. If we take the time to reflect on places people gather, either by choice or out of necessity, we will discover numerous opportunities throughout our day to connect with those we would otherwise never meet.

A great example of this is seen in the life of our friend Dennis. After an unsuccessful surgery to remove a cancerous tumor, Dennis learned that he would need to go through additional radiation treatments every day for eight weeks. He knew right away that the frequency of his radiation treatments would provide possibilities to bring joy and hope to both fellow patients and medical staff, in an environment that is usually full of pain and sorrow. Dennis found himself meeting every day with others in the cancer center, intentionally building relationships, listening to their stories, and providing prayer. As a result, several new relationships were born even in the midst of a huge trial in Dennis' life—all because he saw his treatment journey as a kind of temporary third place.

After considering these different ways of understanding third places there are two specific things we need to be prepared to do.

First: Identify and Incarnate

Third places offer a unique opportunity for missionary-minded people to do life in close proximity to others. But to connect with people in these places of common ground, we must first identify where they are in our community. Where do people gather to spend time with others? Where are the coffeehouses, cafés, pubs, and other hangouts? In some settings these places will be obvious. However, in other neighborhoods you may need to work at identifying these gathering spots.

Once identified, we must seek ways to enter into these places. Incarnational presence involves embedding our lives into a local context. Over time we strive to move from being an occasional visitor to becoming one of the regulars. This issue of frequency is one of the main advantages of building relationships in third places. Your neighbors would probably not appreciate you knocking on their doors every day to say hello and to cultivate a relationship. In fact, you would most likely be considered some type of stalker. But if you frequent a third place every day, you are referred to as a good customer.[2]

Incarnating a place, however, will involve more than simple frequency. We will also need to listen to discover where God is at work. When we listen, we heed the sounds, tune into them, and give consideration to them. The English word *listen* comes from two Anglo-Saxon words, one meaning "hearing" and the other meaning "to wait in suspense."[3]

At least some of our time in public places should be spent hearing our surroundings with an attitude of waiting in suspense. What is it that we are going to hear from the Lord? What are we going to hear from those around us?

Any time I frequent a coffee shop, I try to be sensitive to the surroundings. Simple things like getting to know the baristas, noting the regulars, and listening to the conversations taking place are all important ways of pressing into the setting. It is really the art of noticing. We have to pause, minimize distractions, and become mindful of what is happening around us.

You may need to stop thinking about your third place as a second office, instead thinking of it more as your living room. Remember, third places are *shared* space. Even if you are working in your favorite third place, try to eliminate barriers that might keep people from approaching you and striking up a conversation. In other words, take out your earbuds. There is nothing that says "don't bother me" louder than someone with headphones.

I (Brad) was reminded of this recently while working out at the gym. There was an older gentleman who often exercised at the same time of the day as I did, but I hadn't had an appropriate opportunity to meet him. One afternoon as I saw him walking into the gym—this time with the use of a cane—the Lord prompted me, "Take out your earbuds." I thought, *Wait a minute, I really like this song!* But I took my headphones out and laid my iPhone on the counter. As Scott (I learned his name that day) walked toward me,

I asked him what had happened to his leg. He proceeded to tell me about his knee replacement surgery. Since that day, every conversation Scott and I have at the gym is deepening our relationship. I don't yet know what God is doing through that relationship, but I do know he is doing something that wouldn't have been a possibility if I hadn't listened to the Spirit and listened to Scott instead.

As I shared that story with a friend of mine, he noted that we all have earbuds of some type that keep people at arm's length. What is it for you? When you are in a public place, what hinders your ability to listen? What is it that communicates to others that you want to be left alone? Now of course you might be thinking, *Well, I am more of an introvert, and the truth is I want to be left alone!* So what if you are an introvert? How does that play into starting conversations with strangers? Or getting to know your neighbors?

It is important to be who you are. If God made you an introvert, he just might want you to proceed at an introvert's pace. The truth is, extroverts and introverts bring both strengths and weaknesses to everything we have been discussing in this book.

Extroverts are good at initiating and talking, but often they are not as good at listening and asking the right questions. On the other hand, introverts are good at noticing and watching people, but struggle to initiate conversation. However, once the conversation is initiated, introverts often excel at listening. In fact, a strong argument can be made that introverts are actually better suited for missional conversation—once the difficulty of initiating conversation is overcome—because they would rather ask questions and listen than hear themselves talking.[4]

Second: Be a Place Maker

In addition to identifying third places that already exist in our communities, we will also need to create third-place environments where informal meeting places may not exist. We need to become *place makers*.

The language of place making originated in the 1960s, when activist Jane Jacobs, author of *The Death and Life of Great American Cities*, introduced pioneering ideas about designing cities for people, not just cars and shopping centers. Her work focused on the social and cultural importance of lively neighborhoods and inviting public places.[5] While the concept of place making is much broader than our current discussion on third places, it does provide helpful language when considering taking ordinary space and turning it into meaningful place.

There is actually a place-making movement happening in many cities across the county as it relates to third places. We have several good friends who have opened coffee shops to create a place for community to flourish: Quay's Coffee, Groundhouse, and Post Coffee Company, all in the Kansas City area; Norm's in Newton, Kansas; the Wild Goose Meeting

House in Colorado Springs; Mugs in Little Rock; and Brewed in Fort Worth, just to name a few. In each case the business was started to create a place for people to connect, but in every instance the sense of community has moved far beyond what was initially imagined. There is an abundance of stories of incredible ministry opportunities that have been birthed out of being present in the local community. They are each great examples of place making at its finest.

However, as vital as it is to create new ventures that function as third places in our communities, it is also necessary to consider other simpler approaches. You can turn the simple space of a home patio into a place for weekly cookouts that encourage neighbors to eat together. Or perhaps turn the driveway into an atypical third place by operating a portable fire pit that neighbors gather around for conversation. Westside Family Church, mentioned earlier, has over thirty "fireside" groups where more than three hundred people meet weekly around fire pits. A couple of summers ago, I (Brad) built a permanent fire pit in my backyard, where we can regularly invite neighbors over to make s'mores and hang out. Anytime the neighbors see that we have a fire going, it is a welcome sign to join us.

Being a place maker is simply about creating sweet spots for people to connect. Place really does matter. If we long to see our communities thrive once again, we will need to recognize the importance of third places and discover how to both incarnate into those that already exist and turn ordinary *spaces* into relationally vibrant *places*.

Reflection and Preparation

Immerse. Reflect on the quotation from Oldenburg at the very beginning of this chapter: "Great civilizations, like great cities, share a common feature. Evolving within them and crucial to their growth and refinement are distinctive informal public gathering places." Have you ever thought about the importance of informal public life? Do you have those places in your own life? Can you see the importance they can play in the lives of others?

Recognize your resources. Consider the different types of third places in your community. Where are the typical third places? Make a list, including the name and location of each. Now do the same with the atypical places. Think outside the box. In your community, where are the places you frequent that could serve as an atypical third place? Grocery store? Fitness center? Library? Farmer's market?

Consider others. What will you do to become more in tune with each of these places? How will you be more aware of your surroundings when you enter these third places? In what ways will you be more intentional about engaging these places for the sake of the other?

Pray. Before entering each of the different types of third places mentioned in this chapter, pray that you would be more sensitive to what God is doing in that place. Ask the Spirit to give you not only insight to how he is at work in the lives of others but also the wisdom and courage to lean in to what he is doing.

- 9 -

Treasure Hunt

FINDING THE GIFTS IN YOUR NEIGHBORHOOD

Are we not all books waiting for someone to pick us up
and read the pages that people missed?

SHANNON ALDER

One way of looking at a local block or a small neighborhood is to see it as a
bunch of people with problems and gifts. The job of building community is
to take the problems out of the closet and open up the gifts.

JOHN MCKNIGHT AND PETER BLOCK

FROM THE GOONIES TO JACK SPARROW, to just about
all of us, almost everyone has dreamed of finding long-lost
treasure. In 2013 that is exactly what happened when a
middle-aged couple, out walking their dog on their Northern
California property, made a life-changing discovery. One of
them noticed the top of what looked to be some type of old
canister sticking out of the ground. They dug the container
out with a stick, and back at their house they opened it up,
revealing a stack of dirt-encrusted coins. But these were not
just any old coins. They were perfectly preserved nineteenth-
century twenty-dollar gold coins, minted in San Francisco.
Rushing back to the spot of the discovery, the couple dug up

seven more cans. The total haul was over fourteen hundred coins, later valued at around $11 million.

We are not suggesting you borrow your Uncle Ralph's metal detector and start digging your yard up. But we can say with confidence that there is buried treasure all around you, up and down your street or nearby in your apartment or whatever tenement you live in. The cognitive resources alone are a treasure trove. Add to it the skills, talents, and physical tools and equipment of all sorts present in every neighborhood, and it is legitimate to say that riches surround us.

Most of the assets in our neighborhoods are buried under the scarcity mentality we looked at early on in this book. If you are still reading this deep into the book, we believe that you agree that the scarcity outlook can be broken through. We just need to discover the treasures around us. Literally, we must *dis*-cover them.

Picnic with Jesus

Far from an assumption of insufficiency, Jesus operated from an abundance mentality. All he needed to make wine was some water. He didn't even need the grapes. And he was completely unthreatened by the sight of thousands of hungry people when all he could see before him was a small picnic basket with a little bit of food. Jesus took this opportunity not just to feed people's stomachs but also to feed their (and our) imaginations. This would be a lesson to jailbreak

their thinking from the scarcity pattern to the freedom of
abundance.

> And they went away in the boat to a desolate place
> by themselves. Now many saw them going and
> recognized them, and they ran there on foot from
> all the towns and got there ahead of them. When
> he went ashore he saw a great crowd, and he had
> compassion on them, because they were like sheep
> without a shepherd. And he began to teach them
> many things. And when it grew late, his disciples
> came to him and said, "This is a desolate place, and
> the hour is now late. Send them away to go into
> the surrounding countryside and villages and buy
> themselves something to eat." But he answered them,
> "You give them something to eat." And they said
> to him, "Shall we go and buy two hundred denarii
> worth of bread and give it to them to eat?" And he
> said to them, "How many loaves do you have? Go
> and see." And when they had found out, they said,
> "Five, and two fish." Then he commanded them all
> to sit down in groups on the green grass. So they
> sat down in groups, by hundreds and by fifties. And
> taking the five loaves and the two fish he looked up
> to heaven and said a blessing and broke the loaves
> and gave them to the disciples to set before the
> people. And he divided the two fish among them all.
> And they all ate and were satisfied. And they took up

twelve baskets full of broken pieces and of the fish.
And those who ate the loaves were five thousand
men.

MARK 6:32-44, ESV

Reading through this story, we see the kind of thinking
the disciples operated from is in stark contrast to how Jesus
viewed things. The disciples were functioning from the
common mentality that there is not enough for everyone.
When Jesus told the Twelve to feed the multitude, they
responded incredulously: "Are you kidding? How are we
going to come up with the money to buy enough food for
this crowd?"

The disciples' heads were stuck in a transactional system, which is altogether impersonal. Have you ever gone to
the bank, and when the teller finished your transaction and
asked, "Is there anything else I can do for you?" you said,
"Sure. I'm running a little tight this month. Can you go back
into the vault and get me a couple bundles of Franklins?" I
have wanted to say that so many times to a teller. But the
question is not coming from a personal level, only from a
professional, impersonal level.

The disciples' solution was to send the crowd away to fend
for themselves. The sensible thing to do was for everyone to
strike out on their own, make their way to a local village,
and buy themselves a meal. Let 'em find a Lamburger joint
or Perch-fil-A restaurant. Every man, woman, and family for
themselves.

Jesus had another idea. He says, "*You give* them something to eat." Jesus was working from an understanding that there is more than enough. Peter and the boys wanted the crowd to deal with their own problem. But Jesus was placing the situation at the doorstep of the Twelve. He wanted the disciples to discover a solution beyond the marketplace norm. Purchasing was not the answer here. Giving was.

Notice that Jesus did not ask how much they *needed* to feed the multitude. Jesus didn't ask what was necessary to meet the need. He told them to go and find out how much they had. By doing this, Jesus was not allowing them to languish under their suppositions of scarcity or to just assume they didn't have enough for everyone. He wanted them to inventory what was available so they would see how much they had—which is more than they assumed.

Notice that he didn't ask how many *fish* they had, only *loaves.* The disciples returned from taking stock, and lo and behold, they had more than they thought. Not only did they have some loaves of bread, they also had a couple of fish. Do you think Jesus didn't know that before he sent them to see? This was Jesus at his brilliant best!

The source of the loaves and fishes is revealed in John's account of the incident (John 6:9). A little boy has brought along a sack lunch and has given it toward the task of feeding the community. John also reveals that Andrew got a bit agitated about the entire operation. The small amount of food they had was not going to supply even a crumb-sized portion for each person. Scarcity thinking is like thick morning fog.

It clouds visibility. It dims our capacity to envision greater solutions. But as Walter Brueggemann wrote, "The bread of heaven is a contradiction to the rat race of production."[1]

Individualism and scarcity thinking goes hand in hand. But community and abundance thinking also work together. For example, my next-door neighbor and I (Lance) share lawn-care equipment. Jon and I went in together to buy a lawn mower, I already had a snowblower, and Jon bought a leaf blower and weed trimmer. He has a bigger garage than I do, so we store everything at his place. We share in the care and expense of maintenance for it all. It didn't make sense for each of us to shell out the bucks for all that equipment just to care for a couple of small lots such as ours, and sharing has been a great solution. And the times we do maintenance on our equipment gives us more time to hang out together. Another neighbor in our community recently started a garage gym co-op in his home garage. A group of guys and gals from the neighborhood pooled their workout equipment and created their own fitness spot right in the heart of the neighborhood. They lost the monthly fees and gained neighbor friends.

Okay, back to Jesus' big picnic. Loaves and fishes in hand, Jesus told the disciples to have the people sit down in groups. Don't miss what was happening here. He had them get in clusters of fifty and a hundred—small, community-sized groups. People circled up and closed in together. Jesus then asked God's blessings on the food and began to break the bread and hand it and the fish to the disciples to begin giving to the people. At the end of the meal, twelve full baskets were left over, perhaps one for each disciple to never forget what they had witnessed that day.

We do not want to give the idea that a miracle did not take place. But there seems to be at least something else on a practical level that took place that day. It is reasonable to consider that at least a few people in the crowd witnessed the sharing modeled by the little boy who shared what he had with the disciples, who gave it to Jesus, who in turn blessed it and distributed it to the disciples to pass along to the folks. In any case, this story gives us great lessons for thinking abundantly rather than out of a scarcity mentality.

Opening the Gifts in Our Neighborhoods

Jesus had repositioned the crowd so that, although they themselves *were* the crowd, they didn't *see* a crowd. Gathered in smaller-sized community groups, the people were now face to face in a more cozy setting. They could now see themselves as neighbors within the larger community. Remember the quotation from Mother Teresa from earlier in the book: "I don't see crowds; I see individuals"? When someone takes the initiative to help the community see itself in a smaller, more intimate way, a powerful shift can take place. Jesus helped the people *see* one another.

To recalibrate from scarcity thinking to abundance thinking requires such a shift. In particular, we help our neighbors to recognize each other and our neighborhood to realize its resources. "How many loaves do you have? Go and see," says Jesus. Peter Block speaks to this dynamic:

> The gifts conversation is the essence of valuing diversity and inclusion. We are not defined by deficiencies or what is missing. We are defined by our gifts and what is present. This is so for individuals and communities. Belonging occurs when we tell others what gift we receive from them, especially in this moment. When this occurs, in the presence of others, community is built. We embrace our own destiny when we have the courage to acknowledge our own gifts and choose to bring them into the world.[2]

In consumer culture, what makes for a satisfied life has been distorted. It is believed to be a purchasable commodity. And this feeds scarcity thinking. It is a product of a marketplace and service economy that have constructed such an illusion. Commercialization claims that purchasable systems and products can best fix our day-to-day needs and problems. The problem is that marketplace systems produce answers that always expire and require experts. You have to keep going back to *them* for more and more.

A good metaphor is something Lance's wife has taught us about her seeds of choice for gardening. Most vegetables bought today from large-scale grocery stores are *hybrid* varieties. The upside of hybrids is they can be grown quickly, with a good initial yield. Plus, they have a uniform appearance. They look great on grocery store shelves. The downside is that they have lower nutritional value, are dependent on pesticides, and are not reproducible—you can't save the seeds and plant them for perpetual yields. The everyday gardener cannot develop them. It takes professionals, who grow hybrids in a lab.

Contrast hybrids with *heirloom* vegetables. They are imperfect in appearance, growing in different shapes and sizes. Your heirloom tomatoes are not going to look picture perfect. Plus, you will have a lower initial yield. But here is the payoff: Heirlooms have greater flavor and nutrition, they are drought- and pest-resistant, and they have an exponential harvest, requiring no professional care and expertise.

An abundant neighborhood organizes and structures itself with an *heirloom* mind-set, looking within for its source of a satisfying life. Embracing its own unique diversity, it couldn't care less about uniformity and perfection. If anything, it celebrates its diversity. The variety of gifts, along with the sizes, styles, and shapes of the packages they come in, bring rare beauty to the overall life garden of the neighborhood. Mr. Stevens is a woodworker who fixes furniture and teaches others how to build and repair it. Elizabeth is a fantastic baker and enjoys sharing her recipes and delectable craft with neighbors who want to learn. Debbi and Kent are empty-nesters who invite the neighborhood kids over on a special day each week of the summer to enjoy their pool. Each one of these things can be bought impersonally. You can Google a furniture repair shop, buy a cake at a grocery store, and take the kids to the pool where you have a gym membership. But there is no comparison between the two types of solutions when it comes to relationship and quality. This is the difference between individualism and community, between private and personal. The personal can work in community, while privacy is the domain of professionalized services.[3] A neighborhood with an heirloom mind-set has ceased to outsource the majority of its wants and needs.

When a neighborhood moves from private to personal, the dynamics change. Just this morning, the home of our elderly neighbor from across the street was filled with friends, family, and neighbors who gathered to memorialize his wife, who recently passed away. Grief specialists were not needed. The marketplace sat on the sidelines as the personal serving of neighbors and friends competently cared for one of their own.

What makes a gift a *gift* is that it is given away. Abundant neighborhoods sow the seeds of satisfaction by opening and circulating the gifts of their residents. The primary commodities lining the shelves of such neighborhoods can be summed up in the time they give to and the value they place on kindness, hospitality, cooperation, and generosity. Each of these qualities feeds upon and spurs the other.

Kindness. In an increasingly hostile world, kindness has become rather rare. But this makes it all the more noticeable and desirable when it appears. Kindness is contagious. The more it manifests, the more it catches on and douses the sparks of unkindness. Kindness sets the tone and table for the other goods in an abundance-minded neighborhood.

Hospitality. The welcoming of strangers eventually becomes the welcoming of friends. Houses, garages, front porches, and backyards open up as neighbors share, care, eat with, and teach one another from the abundance of their own individual skills and resources.

Cooperation. Competition, the fuel of the marketplace obsession, peters out in the fields of a cooperative neighborhood. Who wants to keep up with the Joneses when you can hang out with them? Sharing, caring, teaching, learning—these are the pursuits of a functional neighborhood.

Generosity. An economy of generosity is at the heart of an abundant community. Solomon gave us this gem of wisdom in Proverbs 11:25: "A generous person will prosper; whoever refreshes others will be refreshed." This is the system for a non-commoditized community.

Acceptance. The overarching tenor of a neighborhood such as this is its culture of acceptance. It embraces the quirks and oddities that its members bring with them. Marketplace systems churn out hybrid widgets of perfection. Neighborliness cultivates heirloom organics that are rich because of—not in spite of—their distinctiveness.

Treasure Hunt

Some treasure is found by chance. But the really big finds are most often discovered because someone has purposely and actively gone about the task of searching for them. For the pearls of riches in our neighborhoods to be uncovered, someone is going to have to take it upon himself or herself to go about the work of mining them. A friend of ours is someone who has done that very thing—with remarkable results.

Howard Lawrence is a neighborhood miner. In 2013 he set about going door to door in his Highlands neighborhood in northeast Edmonton, Alberta, introducing himself to neighbors and finding out about their hopes and wishes for the neighborhood. He started a neighborhood database, logging what skills, abilities, and gifts his neighbors possessed, plus the hobbies they enjoyed and how they liked to spend their time.

Using his other contacts throughout Highlands, Howard found people who lived on other blocks who were willing to do what he had done on their own blocks. These "block connectors," as he called them, began to cross-pollinate their databases in order to join neighbors with one another per the things they had in common. Strangers quickly became friends as the simplicity of the project started yielding rich rewards. Young mothers began groups to hang out with while their children played together. Guys started playing hockey together. An overarching neighborliness descended upon Highlands. The success of the program was to such a degree that Edmonton hired Howard on a full-time basis to develop block connections throughout the city.

As a friend and colleague of ours with the Forge

Mission Training Network, Howard shared the "Neighbor Conversation Guide" they utilize as block connectors. The survey asks seven questions within three sections:

Part One: Vision for the Highlands Neighborhood

1. What makes a great neighborhood?

2. What else can we do to make the Highlands a great neighborhood?

Part Two: Participating Together in Activities and Interests

3. What activities would you like to join in with neighbors (e.g., oil painting, ball hockey, biking, skiing, bridge, gardening, worship, baseball, jazz guitar, dog walking, animal rescue, gourmet cooking, bird watching . . .)?

4. Do you have interests that you would value discussing or participating in with neighbors (e.g., refugee support, music appreciation, Oilers and Eskimos, art history, philosophy and religion, local food, TED Talks, furniture design, nutrition, politics . . .)?

5. Are there activities or interests with which you are familiar enough to lead in, or teach to, a group of neighbors?

Part Three: Gifts, Abilities and Experiences to Share

6. Do you have a skill, gift, or ability that you would be comfortable using to help neighbors or the neighborhood (e.g., snow shoveling, senior care, cooking, IT, maintenance, gardening, youth mentoring, hospitality, organizing . . .)?

7. Are there some life experiences that you would consider sharing for the benefit of neighbors (e.g., international travel and work, recovery, career path, grief, nurturing, foster or adoptive parenting . . .)?

Anyone could take these questions, or develop a new set, and start connecting neighbors in their own community right away. In our book *The Missional Quest* we shared a set of questions for neighborhood miners to use. The "Reflection and Preparation" section that follows is drawn from that book.

Reflection and Preparation

Our questions revolve around the commandment to love God with our hearts, souls, minds, and strength, and to love our neighbors as ourselves.

What is in your mind? Every street and apartment complex has people living there who know a lot of good stuff about a lot of things. The knowledge reservoir contains understanding and, many times, expertise on a wide range of subjects such as art, math, literature, business, or even neighborhood history.

What is in your hands? This has to do with skill and resources. Musicians, gardeners, bakers, carpenters, and mechanics are abundant in every neighborhood. And they have stuff! They have tools and equipment that they are willing to share with others.

What is in your heart? Most everyone is passionate about one thing or another. Some people are passionate about foster care, saving the environment, or helping stray or abused cats and dogs. Others are interested in community gardens, model railroads, or restoring historic buildings. The list could go on and on. And it does. This is about discovering who cares about what in your neighborhood and helping them connect with others that care about the same things.

Are you willing to teach what you know and share what you have? After we discover the resources and talents in the neighborhood, we will want to find out which people are willing to put up their hands and offer to share their knowledge or possessions with others.

Whom do you know? The saying "It's not what you know but who you know" has validity. There will be instances where certain resources—skill, information, and tools—will not be at the disposal of the neighborhood collective. At the same time, the connections the neighborhood has beyond itself very likely can bring solutions to many of those needs.

Many neighborhoods already have Facebook pages set up that are closed groups. If your neighborhood doesn't have one, you might consider starting one. It may be the simplest place to begin posting the results of your neighborhood survey. Another helpful tool is nextdoor.com, which serves as an online town square. You sign up for your specific neighborhood. Notices of events, opportunities, items for sale or for free, lost-and-found stuff—just about anything that neighbors want to get the word out on—can be posted on the site and e-mailed directly to everyone who has signed up.

Most people are eager and willing to share. All that is needed is someone who is willing to take the initiative to get things started. We suggest getting another person or more to help you if this is something you would like to see happen in your neighborhood. Our neighborhoods are full of gifts just waiting to be opened and shared.

- 10 -

Knocking on Heaven's door

DOING THE STUFF

I dream'd in a dream I saw a city invincible to the attacks
of the whole of the rest of the earth.
I dream'd that was the new city of Friends.

WALT WHITMAN

If our normal, everyday activities rarely coax us out of our private
spheres of home, garage, automobile, and office, how can we build
relationships with those whom we don't already know?

ERIC JACOBSEN, *SIDEWALKS IN THE KINGDOM*

IF YOU ARE THINKING, *Okay, what do I do now?* we hope this chapter will give you some hooks and handles to grab onto and move forward as you express love for your neighborhood and focus on bringing the flavors of heaven to it. Information becomes incarnation only when it is acted upon. Add your hands and feet to the gospel, and it comes alive and interactive. This book will have done you and those around you very little good until you choose to act on it. So we want to leave you with a final chapter that is as practical, adaptable, and doable as possible.

We will try to answer some of the most frequently asked questions we get from folks we meet and work with when we teach and coach others in the joy of neighboring. Plus, we want to provide some ideas that we believe just about anyone can have success in implementing in their neighborhood. As you commence to knock on heaven's door for the sake of our neighborhoods, we first want to encourage you with some scriptural principles. Keep these thoughts in mind as you bring Good News to your neighbors.

God Is Already at Work in Your Neighborhoods

Hanging on the wall in front of my writing desk is a picture of our house in 1940. I (Lance) look at that picture and think, *Seventy-five years ago the Lord was in this neighborhood. My neighborhood.* Way back then, God was seeking to bring compassion, care, peace, and mutual love to our neighborhood. He is still encouraging people to do the same today. That's what prompted us to write this book.

It is no different in your neighborhood. The Lord got there long before you. He is not just passively or distantly observing. In John 5:17 Jesus said, "My Father is always at his work to this very day, and I too am working." God is doing something in your neighborhood. You do not have to talk him into joining you. It should be comforting to know you are joining what he is already doing.

Don't Sweat It

God doesn't need *our* strength. In Galatians 6:9 Paul writes, "Let us not become weary in doing good, for at the proper time we will reap a harvest if we do not give up." The fuel for the good we do is not to be mustered on our own. In fact, Paul said he would rather brag about his weakness than his own strength and stamina; the Lord's grace is more than enough, and his power is perfected in human weakness (2 Corinthians 12:9). We have not come to save our neighborhoods. And we don't bring the Savior to our neighborhoods. We come alongside the Savior.

Our posture must be one of humility and not of a know-it-all nuisance. This is the attitude we need to take with our neighbors. We want them to know that we know we don't have all the answers. Even if we are leading the charge in certain efforts, our attitude must always be that of a learner. Just take it easy and enjoy *living* and loving. Love cannot be forced on anyone. It is a mistake to work *at* love rather than working *from* love. Nehemiah, who was so instrumental in restoring Jerusalem, encouraged the people with the following words: "The joy of the LORD is your strength" (Nehemiah 8:10). Henri Nouwen and his collaborators wrote that

> wherever we see real service we also see joy, because in the midst of service a divine presence becomes visible and a gift is offered. Therefore, those who serve as followers of Jesus discover that they are receiving more than they are giving. Just as a mother does not need to be rewarded for the attention she pays to her child, because her child is her joy, so

those who serve their neighbor will find their reward in the people whom they serve.[1]

When you are praying for something, it is great to already know that it is God's will. Jesus instructed us to pray, "Your kingdom come, your will be done, on earth as it is in heaven" (Matthew 6:10). The Lord wants the will, creativity, economy, and goods of heaven to manifest and be distributed on our spot of earth and our neighbor's spot of earth. When we become aware of a situation in our neighbor's life that is un-heavenly, it means we have come upon a condition to pray the Lord's Prayer over him or her. Consistently praying for your neighbors, by name and with specificity regarding what you know and don't know about the goings-on in their lives, puts you in agreement with the will of heaven for your neighbors.

Common Questions

Here are some the questions people ask most often:

How do I start? The best answer to this question is pretty simple. Begin with what you have. Simply start with what and whom you know. Don't do it alone. It is much more fun and encouraging if you invite others to join you. We can almost guarantee that there is someone else, if not many others, who will jump at the chance to join you in bettering your neighborhood.

An example of this comes from my (Lance's) wife. She decided to do an inventory of her own skills and knowledge one day after talking with Staci, a neighbor who mentioned she didn't know how to break down a whole chicken. Sherri said, "Come over and I'll be glad to teach you. You will save money and you can learn to make your own chicken stock, which is a savings in itself." Staci jumped at the chance. This incident got Sherri to thinking that there are a multitude of lost skills that were known by most women for generations but are somewhat rare nowadays: canning, gardening, raising backyard chickens, sewing, composting, raising backyard honeybees, and so on.

This was the idea seed for starting a monthly gathering called *Forgotten Ways*. The women get together monthly, and someone shares her knowledge and ability, teaching the others the how-tos of a relatively lost skill or art. Men can do a forgotten-ways group too, and they can also teach and learn from the women. Everyone needs to know how to change a car tire and how to monitor and top off the fluids in their engine. Basic carpentry skills and home maintenance are just a few of the things that are helpful for everyone to know.

I've lived here for years and am embarrassed that I don't know my neighbors. How do I introduce myself to someone I've waved to for years? The short answer is, "Just do it." Swallow hard and walk across the street. Let's stop taking ourselves so seriously. We need to gulp down our pride and the bad taste that goes with swallowing it. The small pain we endure in re-introducing ourselves is a tiny price to pay for the possibility of making a fellow resident into a neighbor and friend.

I (Lance) recently reintroduced myself to a couple I met shortly after we moved into our home almost five years ago.

I forgot their names, and we had a gathering coming up that we wanted to invite them to. Glancing out the window one evening, I saw them walking their dog and quickly slipped on a pair of shoes and ran across the street. I decided to just go ahead and eat the crow. "Hi, I'm Lance, from the house on the corner. We met a long time ago, and I'm embarrassed that we never had you over to our home. Can you tell me your names again?" They smiled widely, laughed, and said they felt the same way. Next, I invited them to our gathering, and they happily accepted and showed up. It is clear that a friendship has begun—after almost five years!

How do I reach out to neighbors whose lifestyle I disagree with? In the mode of Jesus, let us answer this question with a question: Did Jesus agree with the lifestyle of the prostitutes, tax collectors, adulterers, and others with whom we see him eating and hanging out throughout the Gospels? Moreover, when did Jesus reach out to you? Did he agree with your lifestyle? If we are talking about more than sexual orientation, does he agree with our lifestyle (consumerism, overindulgence, and the like) right now?

Jesus said he was sent to those who were in need of a doctor, not to the healthy ones. When we shut our lives off from everyone other than our Christian friends, it is tantamount to a hospital only admitting healthy people. Martin Luther King Jr. said,

> Men often hate each other because they fear each
> other, and they fear each other because they don't

know each other. They don't know each other
because they can't communicate with each other;
they cannot communicate with each other because
they are separated from each other.[2]

Our first hurdle is to eliminate the gap of separation.
*"I barely have time enough for myself and my own family.
How do I fit this stuff into my schedule?"* Take a look back at
our chapter on hospitality. In that section we discussed the
importance of margin. Remember, margin is this space that
guarantees sustainability. It is in this space that our batteries are recharged and our relationships are nourished. We
believe this metaphor is helpful when considering the ideas
of neighboring and hospitality because *relationships happen
in the margins.* When there is no margin, it is impossible to
welcome others into our lives.

But how do we do this? Perhaps the two greatest helps
are first to think of *alignment* rather than *addition*. In other
words, don't try to add more activities to your schedule,
but instead look at ways in which you can align your daily
rhythms with the rhythms of life of those around you. And
second, be prepared to prune the activity branches. If you are
serious about creating margin in your life, there will be times
that something will need to be cut off. Furthermore, we must
be reminded that is okay to say no.

I'm an introvert. Help! First off, just be you. The Lord
doesn't call you to be someone you are not. This does not
mean we are not called or designed to touch the lives of

others. It just means we will do so in differing ways. Use what you know and what you know how to do as a connector to others. Look for opportunities to meet others around common interests. When you see those openings pop up, have the discipline to jump on them. These could be hobbies, book-reading groups, gardening groups, or just about anything. The underlying commitment you must make is to refuse to close yourself in. Determine to de-hermitize yourself every chance you get.

How do I reach out to a neighbor I have clashed with? Just about everyone has experienced a certain degree of conflict with a neighbor. It may be that noisy neighbor next door or in the apartment upstairs. Or maybe the neighbor living behind us with the constantly yapping dog. In some instances things get pretty intense between neighbors, to the point where they are not speaking to one another, or worse. Amazingly, there is now a reality television series titled *Fear Thy Neighbor* that chronicles the conflict between neighbors that results in some form of violence, including murder in some cases.

For Christians who are seeking the welfare of their neighborhoods and are trying to love their neighbors, it can be rather daunting when we have had some sort of neighborhood conflict. When this happens we need to take another look at the basics of who we are—our identity as followers of Jesus. We are called to be peacemakers, to bless those who curse us, to offer food and drink to our enemies.

If the kingdom of heaven is going to become tangible,

we must start taking Jesus literally. Make every effort to make peace. The apostle Paul wrote, "If it is possible, as far as it depends on you, live at peace with everyone" (Romans 12:18). Do what you can to extend an olive branch of reconciliation. If the conflict has been over a situation that you can bring peace to by giving in, you can consider allowing yourself to be wronged for the sake of making peace. If you host a meal or event, invite the neighbor you have had issues with, just as you would anyone else.

Try It: You'll Like It

Throughout this book we have told stories and offered examples of what other folks have done in their neighborhoods. This section provides a few more ideas and thoughts for you to consider. Some of these ideas will be something with which you immediately will resonate and feel a lot of confidence in trying. Others may seem a little iffy to you. Big deal! If you try something and it doesn't feel like a fit, no worries. How many times have you gone into a shoe store and tried on a few shoes until you found the right fit? If the shoe fits, wear it. If it doesn't, toss it aside and find another one.

Open up your front yard. For decades my (Lance's) parents had a big three-seat-wide swing and a couple of lawn chairs in their front yard. Literally hundreds of hours were spent over the years in that swing as my mom and dad enjoyed morning coffee or iced tea in the summer evenings. Very often a neighbor—sometimes from a block or so away—would stroll by. Before you knew it, they were swaying in that old swing with a glass of iced tea or a cup of coffee. My folks could just as well have placed the swing in the backyard, where my mom always had beautiful rosebushes and flowerbeds. But they rarely hung out in the backyard. The house was built in the early 1970s—a small suburban tract home with no front porch. I believe that swing had a lot to do with them always knowing so many neighbors, even as the neighborhood turned over throughout the decades as families moved in and out all around them.

If you are interested in ideas on how to make a hangout space in your front yard, check out the DIY network television show *Desperate Landscapes*. It is one of those home-makeover shows that takes something worn down and transforms it into something beautiful. What we find especially intriguing about this show is that, invariably, part of the new landscape design includes an outdoor hangout element. The designer is wonderfully creative in turning front yards into inviting neighborly hangout spots. They become exemplary atypical *third spaces*.

For those who have front porches. If you have a front porch, use it! David Schuyler penned the biography of Andrew Jackson Downing, a noteworthy landscaper gardener from the mid–nineteenth century. Downing's vision for the American home highlighted the front porch as the most significant element, standing apart from English architecture. The front porch offers a transition space, bridging the private world of the family and the public realm of the sidewalk and street. The authors of *The Great Neighborhood Book* write:

Some historians have noted that the gradual shift of outdoor life at home from the front porch to the back patio is a key element in our declining sense of community. Indeed, after World War II, front porches disappeared from houses altogether. They were replaced in many new communities by the dull, blank wall of garage doors.[3]

The loss of front-porch culture is something Kentuckian Claude Stephens is out to change. He is the founder of the Professional Porch Sitters Union Local 1339. In a conversation with CBS News correspondent Steve Hartman, Stephens, whose front porch alias is Crow Hollister, said, "We weren't looking to start anything; it just happened." All he did was post a page on the Internet inviting people to join the Professional Porch Sitters Union and simply "Sit down a spell. That can wait."[4] The word spread, and today there are PPSUs all over the country.

Practice the art of invitation. Invitation is powerful when we stop and think about it. The first part of the word is the word *in*. To invite someone is to include them. It is to take someone from outside to inside. When we get invited to a party, to join others for lunch, or even just to "pull up a chair," something inside of us is touched. It is good to be wanted. When someone invites someone else they are saying, "I need your presence. I don't want you to be an outsider."

One thing that keeps us from inviting others is the anxiety attached to invitation. We are afraid we might get turned down or be stuck with a no-show. As we said earlier: No sweat, no big deal. When doing things in a neighborhood the invitations should have the air of an open-door policy: "If you can make it, great. If not, take a rain check and catch up with us next time." Just make sure to let folks know that even if they can't make it this time, they are always welcome in the future.

To invite others, especially strangers or a person we don't know really well, is to offer the possibility of an alternative future. Most people will be able to pick up on those possibilities, and many will avail themselves of the opportunity. To help with this, it is a good idea to name the possibility. When Lance and his wife sent out their first invitations to a dessert party soon after they moved into their neighborhood, it said, "We just moved here and would really like to get to know our neighbors." When folks showed up that first evening, one thing several of them said was, "I wish we would have done this when we first moved here." They caught the vision because the possibility was emphasized in the invitation.

Little free library. This concept has taken root in a lot of cities; many people claim it as one of the neighborliest things they have ever done. These are little boxes, often designed like little houses, where anyone is welcomed to take a book and share a book for free. Check out https://littlefreelibrary.org.

Game nights. What could be more old school than hosting a regularly scheduled game night? We have all heard about the Texas Hold 'Em phenomenon over the last few years. Poker may not be your game, but there are endless other games. When the weather is good, card games are great for the front porch.

Softball or volleyball. Organize a gender-specific or co-ed team with a roster of neighbors. Game time is fun, and sharing a pizza and drinks afterward is just as much if not more entertaining.

Tool library. Ask neighbors what tools they are willing to share, and post a virtual library of the items and owners on your neighborhood web or social media page.

Holiday parties. Host a neighborhood party for the major holidays. If you only do this at Christmas (or Boxing Day, eh, Canada?), Halloween, St. Patrick's Day, and the Fourth of July, you will be gathering folks together about once a quarter.

Hoop it up. Set up a basketball goal in your driveway. Who doesn't love shooting a few hoops?

Pop-up socials. These are great events to do in a vacant lot in the neighborhood. Invite a few neighborhood vendors or food trucks to come by, or bring your own grill. We have friends that have organized pop-up yoga events, Wiffle-ball games, bean bag tosses, and even pop-up neighborhood farmer's markets. Pop-up dog parks can be created with temporary plastic mesh fencing purchased at your local home center.

Pit stop. Set up a fire pit and watch the magic happen. If you build it they will come!

Start a neighborhood web page. It is very easy to create a closed group on Facebook or to start a page on nextdoor.com. Once you have set it up, go door to door with flyers inviting your neighbors to sign up.

Cul-de-sac salons. This is for the modern suburb. Invite a local hairstylist or two to do haircuts in a home or garage one morning or evening each month. Guys can have a lot of fun with this one.

Fantasy football. Start a league for your neighbors. Hold a special live draft night where everyone hangs out for food and drinks.

Babysitting co-op. This is a no-cost solution that brings neighbors together. Parents "bank" sitting time, and neighborhood children get interaction with one another. See more at www.babysittingcoop.com.

A Final Word

We all long to taste what heaven has to offer. We desire to be in the presence of the Lord. What we so often miss is that his very presence is available right now, through the presence of those made in his image. Jesus said, "When you did it to the least of these, you did it to *me*" (see Matthew 25). Sure, there are times when we encounter God in our times alone—just "Jesus and me." But in the exchange of gifts, talents, skills, goodness, kindness, and grace of others, we experience the bounty of heaven.

Most people just dream of possibilities. Few people take action to bring possibility into tangibility. Our neighborhoods will become livable and sprinkled with the foretastes of heaven only when we decide to act on the little notions, daydreams, and "crazy" ideas running around in our heads. The starting point lies in the word *ownership*. You must own the possibility in your neighborhood. Take ownership and act upon it. The great theologian A. W. Tozer wrote:

> Why do some persons "find" God in a way that others do not? Why does God manifest His Presence to some and let multitudes of others struggle along in the half-light of imperfect Christian experience? Of course the will of God is the same for all. He has no favorites within His household. . . . Pick at random a score of great saints whose lives and testimonies are widely known. Let them be Bible characters or well-known Christians of post-Biblical times. . . . I venture to suggest that the one vital quality which they had in common was spiritual receptivity. Something in them was open to heaven, something which urged them Godward. Without attempting anything like a profound analysis I shall say simply that they had spiritual awareness and that they went on to cultivate it until it became the biggest thing in their lives. They differed from the average person in that when they felt the inward longing they *did something about it*. They acquired

the lifelong habit of spiritual response. They were
not disobedient to the heavenly vision.[5]

Most mornings, one of the first things I (Lance) do after
a cup of coffee has cleared enough cobwebs out of my head
is to spend a few moments praying for our neighborhood
and for the kingdom of heaven to come to bear on the lives
of our neighbors. Pray for heaven to show up. Praying over
our neighbors by name and in light of any current crisis,
concern, or just normal life situation we are aware of keeps
our neighbors' faces and lives on our hearts and constantly at
the throne of God. Just imagine the power of prayer throughout a city, when God's people pray for their neighbors on a
consistent basis.

We urge you to grab hold of Tozer's observation and "do
something about it." Take hold of the heavenly vision and
run with it. If you choose to do so, you and your neighbors
can experience life next door as it is in heaven.

Acknowledgments

From Lance

Thanks to all my friends in Kansas City, my favorite city of all.

Thanks to influencers who became dear friends—such as Hughdog, Alan, Frosty, and Neil.

Thanks to Brad for being the solid rock that you are.

Thanks to inspiring friends such as Ryan and Laura, Geoff and Sherry—those who are giving foretastes of heaven in their neighborhoods.

From Brad

Thanks to Lance for being such a great co-conspirator.

Thanks to my immediate family, including Mischele, Joshua, Caleb, and Chloe, as well as dozens and dozens of foster kids who have come through our home, for helping me to know what it really means to love and be loved. May God continue to guide your every step.

Thanks to Dave Zimmerman—a second time—for being such a great editor.

Thanks to my ministry partners at the North American

Mission Board who allow me to not only resource church planters but to live as a missionary in the great city of Kansas City.

Thanks to Forge America. Because of this very special tribe, I have never been more encouraged for the future of the church in North America. It is a joy to be on this journey with you all.

Notes

INTRODUCTION: THERE GOES THE NEIGHBORHOOD
1. Jay Pathak and Dave Runyon, *The Art of Neighboring: Building Genuine Relationships Right Outside Your Door* (Grand Rapids, MI: Baker, 2012), 20.

CHAPTER 1: PLACE MATTERS
1. Ray Oldenburg, *The Great Good Place: Cafés, Coffee Shops, Bookstores, Bars, Hair Salons, and Other Hangouts at the Heart of a Community* (New York: Marlowe & Company, 1989), xxix.
2. Ibid., 13.
3. Susan Pinker, *The Village Effect: How Face-to-Face Contact Can Make Us Healthier, Happier, and Smarter* (New York: Random House, 2014), Kindle location 212.
4. Gretchen Anderson, "Loneliness among Older Adults: A National Survey of Adults 45+," September 2010, accessed December 31, 2015, www.aarp.org/research/topics/life/info-2014/loneliness_2010.html.
5. Pinker, *The Village Effect*, Kindle location 207.
6. Janice Shaw Crouse, "The Loneliness of American Society," May 18, 2014, http://spectator.org/articles/59230/loneliness-american-society.
7. Steven Bouma-Prediger and Brian J. Walsh, *Beyond Homelessness: Christian Faith in a Culture of Displacement* (Grand Rapids, MI: Eerdmans, 2008), xii, 8.
8. James Howard Kunstler, *The Geography of Nowhere: The Rise and Decline of America's Man-Made Landscape* (New York: Touchstone, 2013).
9. Michael Frost, *Incarnate: The Body of Christ in an Age of Disengagement* (Downers Grove, IL: InterVarsity Press, 2014), Kindle location 153.
10. Eric O. Jacobsen, *Sidewalks in the Kingdom: New Urbanism and the Christian Faith* (Grand Rapids, MI: Brazos Press, 2003), 82.

11. Alan Hirsch, *The Forgotten Ways: Reactivating the Missional Church* (Grand Rapids, MI: Brazos Press, 2006), 133.

12. Simon Carey Holt, *God Next Door: Spirituality and Mission in the Neighbourhood* (Victoria, Australia: Acorn Press, 2007), Kindle location 1399.

13. Jon Huckins and Rob Yackley, *Thin Places: Six Postures for Creating and Practicing Missional Community* (Kansas City: Beacon Hill Press, 2012), Kindle location 594.

14. James Davison Hunter, *To Change the World: The Irony, Tragedy, and Possibility of Christianity in the Late Modern World* (New York: Oxford University Press, 2010), 277.

15. Ibid.

16. Psalm 137 is, in fact, an example of anger directed at Babylonian oppressors.

17. Hunter, *To Change the World,* 277.

18. Ibid., 278.

CHAPTER 2: THE REAL NEIGHBOR

1. Jay Pathak and Dave Runyon, *The Art of Neighboring: Building Genuine Relationships Right outside Your Door* (Grand Rapids, MI: Baker, 2012), 34–35.

CHAPTER 3: YOUR COMMUNITY BANK

1. David Halpern, *Social Capital* (Cambridge, UK: Polity Press, 2005), 2.

2. John McKnight and Peter Block, *The Abundant Community: Awakening the Power of Families and Neighborhoods* (San Francisco: Berrett-Koehler, 2010), 10.

3. Ibid., 10.

4. Peter Block, *Community: The Structure of Belonging* (San Francisco: Berrett-Koehler, 2008), 17.

5. Daniela Drake, "Big Pharma Is America's New Mafia," *The Daily Beast,* February 21, 2015, http://www.thedailybeast.com/articles/2015/02/21/big-pharma-is-america-s-new-mafia.html.

6. Leigh Gallagher, *The End of the Suburbs: Where the American Dream Is Moving* (New York: Penguin, 2013), 40.

7. Ibid., 41.

8. Alan Hirsch and Lance Ford, *Right Here, Right Now: Everyday Mission for Everyday People* (Grand Rapids, MI: Baker, 2011), 161.

9. Gallagher, *The End of the Suburbs,* 13, 68.

10. Robert Putnam, cited in Gallagher, *The End of the Suburbs,* 98.

11. Gallagher, *The End of the Suburbs*, 43.
12. Stephanie Coontz, *The Way We Never Were: American Families and the Nostalgia Trap* (New York: Basic Books, 1992), 25.
13. Elaine Tyler May, cited in Coontz, *The Way We Never Were*, 25.
14. Michael Schluter and David Lee, *The R Factor* (London: Hodder & Stoughton, 1993), 37.
15. Simon Carey Holt, *God Next Door: Spirituality and Mission in the Neighbourhood* (Victoria, Australia: Acorn Press, 2007).
16. Hirsch and Ford, *Right Here, Right Now*, 165.
17. Jon Shirley, "The Desert Blooms: Episode 1," YouTube video, 10:15, posted by "Jon Shirley," July 7, 2014, http://www.youtube.com/watch?v=0qFD7fD7pA0.

CHAPTER 4: HERE COMES THE NEIGHBORHOOD

1. Peter Block, *Community: The Structure of Belonging* (San Francisco: Berrett-Koehler, 2008), 64–65.
2. Ibid., 134.
3. Lance Ford, *Revangelical: Becoming the Good News People We're Meant to Be* (Carol Stream, IL: Tyndale Momentum, 2014), 173.
4. John McKnight and Peter Block, *The Abundant Community: Awakening the Power of Families and Neighborhoods* (San Francisco: Berrett-Koehler, 2010), 37.
5. Walter Brueggemann, *Journey to the Common Good* (Louisville, KY: Westminster John Knox, 2010), 7.
6. Alan Hirsch and Lance Ford, *Right Here, Right Now: Everyday Mission for Everyday People* (Grand Rapids, MI: Baker, 2011), 139.
7. "The Roseto Effect," accessed December 31, 2015, at www.uic.edu/classes/osci/osci590/14_2%20The%20Roseto%20Effect.htm.
8. Rock Positano, "The Mystery of the Rosetan People," November 17, 2011, www.huffingtonpost.com/dr-rock-positano/the-mystery-of-the-roseta_b_73260.html.
9. Ibid.
10. Michael Schluter and David Lee, *The R Factor* (London: Hodder & Stoughton, 1993), 70.

CHAPTER 5: GETTING TO KNOW YOU

1. Alan Hirsch and Lance Ford, *Right Here, Right Now: Everyday Mission for Everyday People* (Grand Rapids, MI: Baker, 2011), 83.
2. Peter Senge, *The Fifth Discipline Fieldbook: Strategies and Tools for Building a Learning Organization* (New York: Doubleday, 1994), 3.

3. Brian Bethune, "The End of Neighbours," *Maclean's*, August 8, 2014, www.macleans.ca/society/the-end-of-neighbours/.
4. Mike Mason, *Practicing the Presence of People: How We Learn to Love* (Colorado Springs: WaterBrook, 1999), 15.
5. Joseph H. Thayer, *Thayer's Greek-English Lexicon of the New Testament* (Peabody, MA: Hendrickson, 1995), s.v. "beholding."
6. Frederick Buechner, *Beyond Words: Daily Readings in the ABC's of Faith* (New York: HarperCollins, 2004), 27. Emphasis in the original.
7. Mason, *Practicing the Presence of People*, 15–16.

CHAPTER 6: NEVER MET A STRANGER

1. James Davison Hunter, *To Change the World: The Irony, Tragedy, and Possibility of Christianity in the Late Modern World* (New York: Oxford University Press, 2010), 245.
2. Elder M. Lindahl, "Face to Face," Summer 2002, accessed December 31, 2015, at www.pietisten.org/summer02/facetoface.html.
3. Steven Garber, *Visions of Vocation: Common Grace for the Common Good* (Downers Grove, IL: InterVarsity Press, 2014), 115.
4. Daniel Homan and Lonni Collins Pratt, *Radical Hospitality: Benedict's Way of Love* (Brewster, MA: Paraclete, 2001), xxii.
5. Simon Carey Holt, *God Next Door: Spirituality and Mission in the Neighbourhood* (Victoria, Australia: Acorn Press, 2007), Kindle location 342–344.
6. Alan Hirsch and Debra Hirsch, *Untamed: Reactivating a Missional Form of Discipleship* (Grand Rapids, MI: Baker, 2010), 166.
7. Richard A. Swenson, *Margin: Restoring Emotional, Physical, Financial, and Time Reserves to Overloaded Lives* (Colorado Springs: NavPress, 2004), 77.
8. Richard Swenson. *The Overload Syndrome: Learning to Live within Your Limits* (Colorado Springs: NavPress, 1998), Kindle location 88–89.
9. Richard Swenson, *A Minute of Margin: Restoring Balance to Busy Lives— 180 Daily Reflections* (Colorado Springs: NavPress, 2003), Kindle location 207–215.
10. Swenson, *The Overload Syndrome*, Kindle location 124–128.
11. Arthur Sutherland, *I Was A Stranger: A Christian Theology of Hospitality* (Nashville: Abingdon Press, 2006), 83.
12. Swenson, *Margin*, 122.
13. Anne Lamott, cited in Richard A. Kauffman, "Wisdom for Ministry," *Christianity Today*, November 1, 2003, 75.

14. John Ortberg, *The Life You've Always Wanted: Spiritual Disciplines for Ordinary People* (Grand Rapids, MI: Zondervan, 1997), 81.
15. Alan Fadling, *An Unhurried Life: Following Jesus' Rhythms of Work and Rest* (Downers Grove, IL: InterVarsity, 2013), 78.
16. Ibid., 173.
17. Henry G. Brinton, *The Welcoming Congregation: Roots and Fruits of Christian Hospitality* (Louisville, KY: Westminster John Knox, 2012), 124.

CHAPTER 7: MEALS ON HEELS
1. Robert Karris, *Eating Your Way through Luke's Gospel* (Collegeville, MN: Liturgical Press, 2006), 14.
2. Guy Trebay, "Guess Who Isn't Coming to Dinner," *New York Times*, November 28, 2012, www.nytimes.com/2012/11/29/fashion/saving-the -endangered-dinner-party.html?_r=0.
3. "Are Dinner Parties a Thing of the Past?" accessed December 31, 2015, www.thekitchn.com/are-dinner-parties-a-thing-of-the-past-181185.
4. Michelle Jamrisko, "Americans' Spending on Dining Out Just Overtook Grocery Sales for the First Time Ever," April 14, 2015, www.bloomberg .com/news/articles/2015-04-14/americans-spending-on-dining-out-just -overtook-grocery-sales-for-the-first-time-ever.
5. Kerisha Harris, "Cooking: The Life Skill That Everyone, Except Young People, Loves to Hate," October 17, 2014, http://fusion.net/story/21225 /for-millennials-theres-still-some-joy-in-cooking/.
6. Eugene Peterson, *Christ Plays in Ten Thousand Places: A Conversation in Spiritual Theology* (Grand Rapids, MI: Eerdmans, 2005), 214.
7. Ibid., 214–215.
8. Leonard Sweet, *From Tablet to Table: Where Community Is Found and Identity Is Formed* (Colorado Springs: NavPress, 2014), 5.
9. Philip Yancey, *What's So Amazing about Grace?* (Grand Rapids, MI: Zondervan, 1997), 19.

CHAPTER 8: HANGOUTS
1. Ray Oldenburg, *The Great Good Place: Cafés, Coffee Shops, Bookstores, Bars, Hair Salons, and Other Hangouts at the Heart of a Community* (New York: Marlowe & Company, 1989), 22–42.
2. This idea was originally articulated by our friend Scott Pixler.
3. Lynne M. Baab, *The Power of Listening: Building Skills for Mission and Ministry* (Lanham, MD: Rowman & Littlefield, 2014), 5.
4. Greg Finke, *Joining Jesus on His Mission: How to Be an Everyday Missionary* (n.p.: Tenth Power Publishing, 2014), Kindle location 114.

5. Project for Public Spaces, "What is Placemaking?" accessed December 31, 2015, www.pps.org/reference/what_is_placemaking/.

CHAPTER 9: TREASURE HUNT

1. Walter Brueggeman, *Journey to the Common Good* (Louisville, KY: Westminster John Knox, 2010), 18.
2. Peter Block, *Community: The Structure of Belonging* (San Francisco: Berrett-Koehler, 2008), 17.
3. John McKnight and Peter Block, *The Abundant Community: Awakening the Power of Families and Neighborhoods* (San Francisco: Berrett-Koehler, 2010), 69.

CHAPTER 10: KNOCKING ON HEAVEN'S DOOR

1. Donald McNeill, Douglas A. Morrison, and Henri Nouwen, *Compassion: A Reflection on the Christian Life* (New York: Doubleday, 1982), 32.
2. Martin Luther King Jr., "Towards Freedom," speech at Dartmouth College, May 23, 1962, accessed December 31, 2015, www.dartmouth .edu/~mlk/atdartmouth/towardsfreedom.html.
3. Jay Walljasper and Benjamin Fried, *The Great Neighborhood Book: A Do-It-Yourself Guide to Placemaking* (Gabriola Island, BC: New Society, 2007), 48–49.
4. Michelle Singer, "Professional Porch Sitters Unite," August 17, 2007, www .cbsnews.com/news/professional-porch-sitters-unite/.
5. A. W. Tozer, *The Pursuit of God* (Camp Hill, PA: Christian Publications, 1982), 66–67. Emphasis added.

About the Authors

Brad Brisco is church-planting strategist for a network of churches in Kansas City. He holds a doctorate in the area of missional ecclesiology and has taught college-level courses for more than ten years. Brad blogs regularly at missionalchurchnetwork.com.

Lance Ford is a writer, coach, and consultant with over two decades of experience in pastoral and church-planting ministry. He holds a master's degree in global leadership from Fuller Theological Seminary and is an adjunct professor at Biblical Theological Seminary. He is the author of several books, including *Right Here, Right Now* (with Alan Hirsch); *Unleader*; and *Revangelical*.

Together, Lance and Brad have written two books: *Missional Essentials* and *Mission Quest*. They train and consult with churches and denominations throughout the United States, and they serve together on the national leadership team for the Forge America Missional Training Network.

practices to the question of how to foster good news in our own streets and local neighborhoods. They offer invaluable wisdom for any Christian or local church that is serious about neighborhood transformation rather than just tinkering with Sunday worship. Bring on a new era of living and serving locally!

DARREN CRONSHAW

Mission catalyst, Baptist Union of Victoria; and professor of missional leadership, Australian College of Ministries